HOW TO
GET GOING
WHEN YOU CAN BARELY
GET OUT OF BED

PRENTICE HALL PRESS • NEW YORK

Published in 1987 by Prentice Hall Press
A Division of Simon & Schuster, Inc.
Gulf + Western Building
One Gulf + Western Plaza
New York, NY 10023

Originally published by Prentice-Hall, Inc.

PRENTICE HALL PRESS is a trademark of Simon & Schuster, Inc.

Library of Congress Cataloging-in-Publication Data
Bailey, Linda J.
　How to get going when you can barely get out of bed.

　Includes index
　1. Depression, Mental.　2. Women—Mental health.
I. Title.
RC537.B333　　1984　　159′.1　　83-24752
ISBN 0-13-407304-5 (pbk.)

Manufactured in the United States of America

13　12　11　10　9　8　7　6　5　4

First Prentice Hall Press Edition

To Jessica Marie Bailey,
born and died 1983.
Beloved daughter and relentless teacher
of personal power, acceptance, and integrity—
who forced me to put this material to the test.

Contents

Preface

The two purposes of this book are reflected in two distinct sections. Part I explores the problem of depression, which happens to the human psyche when we forfeit or lose touch with our power. Part II is a comprehensive practical approach to working with depression, building self-confidence, and developing direction and motivations through down-to-earth information and a wide selection of powerful (though often deceptively simple) exercises; the reader will be able to "get going" by overcoming a variety of psychological stumbling blocks in order to reclaim personal power and move onward toward the growth of the spirit.

This is also a book about women. It is not, however, specifically about women. Rather, it is generally about women and all human beings as well. Since its inception, psychology has defined the male experience as normative, and yet who would define general psychology or Freudian theories as the psychology of men? Based on my experience in private practice as well as personal experiences, it has become clear to me that the issues of power, helplessness, and depression are simply more familiar to women. True, this may be because women are thought to be more in touch with their feelings. But there are also many components of the female sex role that predispose them to these problems. But, of course, many men are all too familiar with depression and feelings of helplessness. It is not a matter of exclusivity, but rather proportion, that has caused me to focus on the female experience of powerlessness.

And so this is not a book just about women; rather, it is a book about human beings, in which the female experience is considered normative. Men will benefit from it greatly, in increasing their understanding of women, but, more importantly, in understanding their own quest for personal power as well as their disowned feminine aspects. The route to the problem may differ somewhat in each sex, but the problem itself and the search for its resoluton is a consistent, universal, and wholly human struggle for personal power.

ACKNOWLEDGMENTS

There are many people who have contributed time, energy, and encouragement to the creation of this book.

I would like to thank my mother, Agnes Bailey, who through our many conversations has inspired this book as well as my work in psychology and women's studies. I appreciate her unwavering encouragement and her exceptional mind.

My father, George Bailey, has blessed me with the courage to commit my beliefs to paper and gave me an unusually non-sexist upbringing that has allowed me to pursue the development of my potential.

My grandmother, Marie Doyle, was my earliest writing teacher. She has served as a role model throughout my life and will continue to do so. It is her belief in me that has carried me through the difficult moments.

Bill Womack and Roy Bullock helped me create the bridge between my own experience and the experience of others through communications and psychology.

There are a group of people who helped me translate a painful period of my life into this book. Through their healing energy I have been able to reestablish an abandoned career, overcome a maze of obstacles, learn the message of pain, and approach life creatively. These people are: Troy Scott, Mili Kari, Bob Marrone, Dolores Brubeck, James Reichle, Debbie Brooks, and Jimmy Durbin. Thanks for "hanging in there" with me.

I would also like to thank my editor, Mary Kennan, for her perfect sense of timing in providing me a much needed opportunity.

Sherry Anderson, Dio Neff, and Carol Schlussler did the typing of this book and contributed invaluable suggestions as well. For this I am deeply grateful.

I would like to thank all my courageous clients and students who have proven to me over and over that the problem of depression *can* be overcome.

Finally, I would like to express my love and appreciation to Gary Schlussler, who like a dedicated Lamaz father, truly coached me through the birthing process of this book.

The definition of *power* on page 4 and of *apathy* on page 94 are reprinted with permission from *The American Heritage Dictionary of the English language.* ©1981 Houghton Mifflin Company.

The excerpts from *Unfinished Business* by Maggie Scarf—copyright ©1980 by Maggie Scarf—are reprinted by permisison of the author, Doubleday & Company, Inc., and Candida Donadio & Associates.

Excerpts from *Depression and the Body* by Alexander Lowen—©1972, Alexander Lowen, M.D.—are reprinted by permission. Coward, McCann & Geohegan is the publisher of the hard cover edition.

Excerpts from *Gestalt Self Therapy* by Muriel Schiffman are reprinted by permission of the author.

Excerpts from *The Courage to Live* by Ari Kiev, M.D.—copyright ©1979 by Ari Kiev, M.D.—are used by permission of Bantam Books, Inc. All rights reserved.

Excerpts from *The Universal Traveler* by Don Koberg and Jim Bagnall—copyright ©1976, 1981 by William Kaufmann, Inc.—are reprinted with permission. All rights reserved.

The excerpts "The Objects of Love" are from pages 46-47 of *The Art of Loving* by Erich Fromm, Volume 9 World Perspectives Series, edited by Ruth Nanda Anshen. Copyright ©1956 by Erich Fromm. Reprinted by permission of Harper & Row, Publishers, Inc. and George Allen & Unwin (Publishers) Ltd.

The excerpt from page 77 of *The Spiral Dance: A Rebirth of the Ancient Religion of the Great Goddess*—copyright ©1979 by Miriam Simos—is reprinted by permission of Harper & Row, Publishers, Inc.

The excerpts from "Witchcraft and Women's Culture" by Starhawk in *Womanspirit Rising: A Feminist Reader in Religion* edited by Carol P. Christ and Judith Plaskow—copyright ©1979 by Carol P. Christ and Judith Plaskow—are reprinted by permission of Harper & Row, Publishers, Inc. and the author.

PART ONE

chapter one

Early Lessons

THE NAMING
OF THE PROBLEM

I knew the problem well but lacked its title, like a familiar but nameless smell. I could sense the problem in the lives of my clients in my counseling practice. I was all too aware of the problem in myself as well. I had observed its cancerous, consuming energy as it ate at the ambition and peace of the lives of so many people, both women and men . . . but mostly women. I was sure the problem had something to do with feeling stuck, helpless, and emotionally paralyzed.

For a while I defined the problem as depression. Though depression was the correct clinical term, I felt it to be a too narrow and superficial description. Depression is also a deceptive term, as many people who are depressed do not realize it. The more I read about depression, the more I sensed that I had yet to find the right perspective.

One evening I sat down with my dictionary and a list of

words that were my clues to this search. I looked up depression, helplessness, apathy, and fear—all feelings connected with the problem—but I learned nothing new. Maybe, I wondered, the problem wasn't any of these feelings, but rather the absence of another feeling.

I looked up the word "power," and as I read these words, the pieces of the puzzle fell into place. "Power is the capacity to act or perform effectively." Within that moment, I understood the meaning of this book, my struggle with myself, and the common thread of all my work. The therapy I do with others, the assertiveness training and self-confidence building I teach, as well as this book, all came together with one intent, one purpose: to help others reclaim their innate personal power. All emotional problems, all neurotic behaviors, all family and social problems, hold in common the issue of personal power. People may forfeit their power to others or negate their own power or seek to regain power through destructive means. People may choose to numb the pain of their disowned power or attempt to regain their power vicariously through associating with powerful people. In extreme circumstances, people may seek to regain power over their own lives by forcing their will on others. In equally extreme circumstances, people may seek to regain power over their lives in the last desperate act of suicide.

Wherever the road of powerlessness and helplessness leads us, the end result is that of wasted lives, deadened by lost hope and endless frustration and grief. The cure is not easy, quick, or painless. But it can be done if we are fully committed to healing old wounds, weaning ourselves of our addictions and dependencies, as well as facing those frightening but important lessons and feelings we have so long avoided.

In my work as a counselor I have seen that there is a large difference between understanding a problem and the ability to take action to resolve the problem. In working with women's problems and, more specifically, the problem of helplessness, the ability to take action is of prime importance. Awareness is not only not enough, but, without action, it is sometimes destructive. Awareness often fools us into thinking we have solved the problem, that we have indeed taken action—when we have not. Also, awareness without the ability to take the appropriate action can cause depression in and of itself. This is the concept from which the colloquialism, "ignorance is bliss," was coined.

This book stresses the need to balance awareness with action. Understanding our helplessness and depression as a woman's problem is important. It is important, too, that we understand our role in our culture and understand the myths, values, and stereotypes that are projected onto us. This helps us know we are not alone, that there is a "normalness" to our problem. It also helps us to understand the reactions of others when we begin to break out of the norm and truly lead our own lives.

No amount of understanding helplessness and depression will lead us to break out of it without concrete action. Action is living. It is dynamic and forceful. Helplessness is the postponement of living. It is passive and depressive. Action is constructive. Helplessness is deadly. No matter how well we intellectually understand the problem, nothing can take the place of the day-to-day action. This is the private battle that we must wage daily to overcome helplessness and depression in our lives. This is the *only* route to our lost sense of personal power . . . to reclaim our capacity to act in our own behalf, effectively, confidently, and toward our growth and happiness. This battle is a long one, a quiet, subtle battle of decisions, actions, and emotions. But it is not an endless battle or a futile one. Through it we can free ourselves from the tyranny of depression and helplessness and regain our dignity, strength, and power to recreate our world.

CONCEPTION

In the beginning, there was security, warmth, and darkness; our needs were met by Mother. There was no desire or frustration, only completeness and fulfillment. Then we were expelled, stolen from our safety. During what is known of as birth, we struggled against death and discovered fear. In this new world our needs were met, but not automatically. Sometimes our needs were anticipated and, when this happened, we felt secure and loved. Sometimes our needs were ignored and we felt abandoned and afraid. For a while we recognized no one but Mother and it seemed difficult to determine where Mother ended and we began. Eventually we learned this separateness and we learned loneliness as well. We learned to win Mother's smile and later, as we began to explore all the many, wondrous things around us, we learned to fear Mother's anger. Soon we knew our name and our sex as well. For the rest of our lives, we would continue to learn the meaning of being female or male.

If we received the physical and emotional nurturing we needed as well as encouragement toward independence and competence, then we willingly let go of childhood and eagerly tackled the responsibility of adulthood. If we were in some way deprived of any one of these important elements, then we became emotionally handicapped, faced with two conflicting desires to move forward and to retreat, to become independent adults and yet to remain dependent children. Most of us faced this conflict, the walking wounded of an unbalanced childhood, which stressed either too much nurturing and dependence or too much independence and achievement. Deprived of our innate sense of personal power and adequacy, we find ourselves dragging through life with grim determination, seemingly unable to find fulfillment, joy, or the key to a happier way of life.

We ask ourselves, "What's the use?" and remind ourselves that most people aren't happy. We give up in some very fundamental way and settle for the mundane boredom but no pain, safety but no fulfillment. We con ourselves into believing that the absence of pain is happiness. We kill the pain of this incredible sense of absence and loss with compulsive activity, television, alcohol, sleep, and drugs.

Somewhere, somehow, the pain seeps through, relentlessly reminding us that we are living a lie. During those overwhelmingly painful moments, we feel as if we are drowning, sinking into an abyss of fear, loneliness, self-hate, and grief. The rest of the time, when those moments have been carefully rationalized and buried, we manage just to tread water. It takes all our energy to stay afloat, but we sense we are making no progress. And so our sense of frustration heightens and our grief deepens, as more and more the desire to give up, to not care anymore, seductively beckons us. Occasionally, we move a bit forward, meeting a goal, and for a while our hope soars and we begin to believe that all is solved. But soon the movement seems insignificant compared to the huge, dead ocean that surrounds us. Our real goals and desires seem impossible. So the feelings of desperation return, and we are lost once again.

This is depression; the absence, the loss of meaning, the feelings of helplessness and grief, guilt and fear, as well as the strong capacity to ignore or deny all these painful feelings. Depression, an emotional "dis-ease" that can span a lifetime, often goes unrecognized in the individual (or even by a helping professional) and is becoming an American epidemic. Depression is "treated" by individuals via bars, divorce courts, television, drugs, and chronic illnesses. Depression masquerades as alcoholism, child abuse, underachieving, overachieving, and many forms of violence as well.

The energy needed to fight depression is enormous. This continual draining of energy resources causes us to feel tired, irritable, nervous, lacking in true sexual desire, and without the ambition to pursue our goals. Depression is found in four to ten times more women than men. This book attempts to solve the Why? to that statistical riddle as well as give practical self-help approaches to healing ourselves of the habits, thoughts, and predispositions of depression.

SELF-IMAGE, MYTHS, AND VALUES

Self-image is the single most powerful influence in our lives. This is how we imagine ourselves to be, a distillation of our past experiences with others compounded with our idealized self. The idealized self is what we think we should be and, to some extent, what we hope to be. Combine the idealized self with all the impact of our lives, the past experiences, relationships with others, feedback from our intimate relationships, and we have self-image.

Self-image has so powerful an influence on our lives because, as human beings, we tend to seek security from consistency and therefore create lives via decisions to be consistent with our self-image. Though the self-image is, to some extent, constantly in flux, it seems that the self-image is quite resistant to significant change. We tend to live our lives to be consistent with self-image no matter what the cost.

Self-image is so strong that it actually affects incoming information so that we filter out that which we do not recognize or is inconsistent with self-image. This is why, in a problem situation, we often see only one or two alternatives when there are many. Self-image also affects our communication, including how we present ourselves, our vocal-tone, our choice of words, our "body language," all of which affect our relationships and the course of our lives.

Myths and values greatly affect the developing self-image. Myths and values reflects the "shoulds" of a society. A value is simply a belief or belief system that is considered valuable by an individual or society. A myth is a parable that reflects a society's values. Myths are not only stereotypes, but fantasies about what happens to those stereotypic people, fantasies that are often accepted as predictable reality if the values reflected in the myth are consistent with the values of the individual or culture. Since children have no experience to make judgments regarding which myths are real, we tend to believe all myths that we are presented with during childhood unless we are told a specific myth is not real, at which point we usually (though sometimes reluctantly) give up our belief in the myth. Some myths are quite evident, like Santa Claus or the idea that "any one can be president." Other myths are subtle, but their message is strong due to its repetition, as in "a woman who is a high achiever will end up bitter and alone."

Some myths reflect values of "shoulds" that become incorporated into our self-image as assumptions. Assumptions are belief systems that are so well integrated into our lives and self-image that we no longer ever consider questioning these beliefs. In a sense, assumptions are no longer simply beliefs, rather, they are "truth" as we know it. Mother tells us not to touch the iron because it is hot and will burn us. Eventually, we believe her, possibly after experimentation. Soon we assume an iron is hot. Later, we will learn an iron is not always hot and so we will change our assumptions about irons. The assumption is usually changed only when we are forced to test it or faced with irrefutable proof. Many assumptions are never tested again after they are acquired in childhood. When they are challenged and are changed, our self-image changes as does our view of the world.

Myths, values, and assumptions all help to determine who

we are and our relationships to the world. These factors make the decisions that direct the course of our lives, all those decisions we make on a day-to-day and moment-to-moment basis. These myths, values, and assumptions are passed onto us by our family, our culture (and subcultures), and the media. Through our experiences with family, culture, subcultures, and media, we develop as individuals. This development is a continuous process. We no more arrive at a point when we are whom we will be for the rest of our lives than we arrive at a point when we are "together." The personality is constantly in process, very slowly changing. Our basic assumptions, though, tend to remain fairly constant. Overall, the personality changes in fairly small ways as the individual matures. Larger scale changes tend to take place due to crisis, therapy or, in some cases, circumstances due to some accident or "fate."

People generally seek major changes in their lives only because they are in intolerable pain. In this way, pain can be seen as a good thing, a vehicle or alarm that tells us that we must make some changes. Our problems become compounded when we ignore our pain and thereby lose its message. Once we have learned to ignore pain, we become like people who have had their nerve endings damaged or severed. If we cut ourselves, we have not one but two problems. First, that we are bleeding and, second, that we don't know that we are bleeding. The first problem can be remedied by a few stitches. The second problem can be fatal. This analogy is a good description of helplessness and the denial of unpleasant feelings so common in depression, which not only makes it difficult to solve our other problems, but becomes a problem in and of itself. It is this second problem, the inability to act due to helplessness and denial of feelings, that is the root of depression. And it is this problem, this sense of personal paralysis, that is actually familiar to women.

LESSONS IN FEMININITY

Our earliest sense of ourselves is based on our sexuality. We are either female or male from the moment of conception. From a purely biological basis, our sexuality probably has little effect on our personalities. But each culture develops definitive expectations of how females or males should act. Though some cultures studied by anthropologist Margaret Mead show a reversal of Western sex roles, very few cultures have uniform expectations of women and men. It seems that society needs to delegate certain traits to one sex or the other, though what traits are assigned to which sex is apparently an arbitrary process. In most cultures we see a pattern of the traits of nurturing assigned to women, while aggression is assigned to men. These trait assignments are based on the obvious biological differences of the sexes, where women have the capacity to bear children and men tend to be larger than women in stature. But we cannot assume that these biological differences cause these traits. Not all women are nurturing and not all men are aggressive. Males do show nurturance and females do show aggression as well. Some sociologists and anthropologists speculate that this division of traits was necessary and helpful at the early beginnings of the evolution of human society. Since the infant mortality rate must have been enormous, it made sense for human society to encourage nurturing behavior in females in order to teach them proper child care and better insure the continuation of the species or clan. Since dangers were plentiful, someone had to protect the tribes most precious valuables (namely, the children), and, through an obvious process of elimination as well as the acknowledgment of size, men were appointed the roles of aggressor and protector. And so, sex roles began.

Today, in this culture, females are trained to be feminine; namely, helpless, weak, nurturing, helpful, endearing, subservient, and very concerned about physical appearance (no doubt part of the method to be endearing). Males are likewise trained to be masculine; namely, strong, active, competent, and aggressive. The feminine domain is that of feelings and the home. The masculine domain is that of logic and the outer world. There is no doubt that the male sex role has its negative side effects, including an alienation from emotions that inhibits their ability to express themselves and which can cause poor relationships with others, stress-related physical disease, and a high rate of alcoholism, drug abuse, suicide, and antisocial behavior. But, if the male sex role is destructive, the female sex role is devastating, eliminating almost all the natural personality traits necessary for effective human functioning or exaggerating those few positive traits allowed to us to such an extreme that these too become liabilities rather than assets.

In comparison to the masculine sex role, the feminine sex role is very limited, allowing only a small range of so-called acceptable behaviors. "Boys will be boys" allows much latitude in behavior and beyond traditionally masculine behavior, males are valued for being sensitive, cooperative, and good fathers. Females are not given such a wide realm of acceptable behavior. So-called "negative" behaviors such as displays of anger, stubbornness, loudness, and rough play are not tolerated in girls. Girls are rarely admired for being aggressive, highly achievement-oriented, or independent. Though feminine behavior is considered a bonus to a basically masculine male, as long as it is not excessive to the point of being submissive, masculine behavior in a female somehow makes her pitiable and definitely less than desirable. Consider, for example, the girl who always makes straight A's. She may be praised for her achievement, yet we fear she will not be marriageable material *because* of her intellectual talent. But we assume a boy with straight A's will go far as a male and as a provider. The female must walk a straight, narrow, tightrope of behavior in order to be feminine, a role which becomes narrower and more restrictive with time. If she exemplifies feminine behavior, she is "good;" if she exemplifies masculine behavior she is "bad." This "either/or" aspect of the feminine role is reflected in the nursery rhyme that goes, "There was a little girl who had a little curl right in the middle of her forehead. And when she was good, she was very, very good. But when she was bad she was horrid."

Many, if not all of the aspects of the female sex role, and all that we call femininity, sets the stage for depression, as well as an inability to efficiently and effectively solve problems. Females are encouraged to be helpless and dependent through being over-protected and overhelped. Girls "have it easy" throughout childhood by not being encouraged or forced to take on responsibility, by being protected from fear-inducing situations, and inhibited from testing their physical capacities. Female babies are often overly gratified, in that their mothers quickly and consistently respond to their cries. When Johnny cries from fear or a fall, Mother is not so quick to come running, which teaches Johnny to deal with frustration and face life's problems on his own. Johnny learns he can trust his own resources and his ability to survive. His sister, Sally, learns to distrust herself, to be dependent on others, and to fear for her capacity to survive without help from others.

Johnny plays with toys that enable him to develop his skills and self-confidence. Johnny proudly sees a tangible result from his efforts as he builds a bridge with his erector set or finishes his birdhouse. He is not dependent on others to acknowledge his accomplishments because the evidence is clearly before him. Sally must content herself with imaginary tasks and scenarios with her dolls. She cooks imaginary meals and dresses her Barbie doll for imaginary dates with Ken. Generally, she finds such activities boring and finds interacting with adults much more entertaining. She uses her perceptiveness to charm adults into providing her the acknowledgment she so desperately needs in lieu of the sense of competence and independence that her brother has developed.

She learns to be helpful, to assist Mother in household duties; and this makes her feel important for a few moments, at least. But meals disappear, and a clean house soon becomes messy and all too soon her achievements have disappeared. So she becomes more and more dependent on the compliments and proud smiles of her parents. Soon she is expert at soliciting parental approval. She will learn to be charming, helpful, cute, and helpless to gain their attentions. When she fails to elicit this parental approval, she will assume that she just isn't "good enough." Slowly, the natural need to achieve and gain self-respect through independent action will weaken and be replaced with dependency and approval seeking. Her sense of self-worth will soon be based totally on what others think of her, rather than who she is. In fact, there will come a time when she may find herself unable to distinguish her values, needs, thoughts, and feelings from the values, needs, thoughts, and feelings of those she loves. In effect, through her addiction to seeking approval, she will lose her self-confidence and, through her dependency, she will lose identity.

So we have a young girl trained to be subservient, compliant, dependent, endearing, helpless, and helpful. Her desire to achieve in tangible terms has been more or less extinguished as she has been discouraged from facing the frustration and risk taking necessary to achieve. The capacities necessary to meet her own needs, solve her own problems, face conflict, make her own decisions, trust in her personal power and strength, will remain underdeveloped and eventually atrophy.

All humans need hope, a goal, a direction to gain happiness, and a sense of importance. The female is presented with a hope, a vehicle by which she may remain or become the loved and pampered princess she has learned to desire. This hope is modeled by her father, the bestower of power, who is symbolized by the messiah-like Prince Charming and graphically defined by Colette Dowling in *The Cinderella Complex*. Along with this fantasy fed to her in the form of a realistic goal will come a threat to ensure that she takes the properly prescribed route. This threat is known as The Boogie Man. Through her lessons in femininity, she has been trained to forfeit her capacity to act in her own behalf or create the life she desires, an education which will predispose her to depression.

chapter two

Big Daddy, Prince Charming, and the Boogie Man

Early in her development, the female is exposed to the notion that her life will not truly begin until she meets The Man, otherwise known as Prince Charming. At first, of course, she has a man—Daddy. Daddy to some extent, either overtly or covertly, rules the roost. If Daddy is missing, either through death or divorce, her search for The Man will begin early and often prove frustrating. If Daddy is around a lot and very attentive, her search will begin much later. If Daddy is a weekend Daddy who lavishes gifts and affection, she may never be content with another man who has real limits and imperfections. If Daddy is affectionate and open when she is a girl, but withdraws with the onset of her puberty, she will learn that her sexuality is something negative that causes loss of love, and that men are not to be trusted emotionally or sexually.

Beyond her relationship with her real Daddy, through books, fairy tales, the media, and the impact from those around her, she will learn about Prince Charming, The Man who will magically begin her life and solve all of life's problems. It will be Prince Charming who will make her whole, who will give meaning and form to her life, who will appreciate and love her. He will tell her what to do with her time so that she will feel competent and important. She will realize that being cooperative, flirtatious, attractive, and nurturing are all skills learned for the purpose of catching and keeping this Prince. She believes that this Prince will protect her from the Boogie Man and the other problems of life. The Prince will become what her parents have been, protectors and providers, who will enable her to continue her childhood dependency, while helping her avoid the issue of autonomy and independence. The Prince will soothe her fears so she will not have to face them. He will tell her what he likes so she will not have to learn her own desires. She will live her life through him so that she will not need to take the responsibility for living her own.

So, as this child begins to face the normal and natural conflicts of childhood, i.e., autonomy, independence, morality, responsibility, etc., she learns through a multitude of myths that she doesn't really have to face any of these problems at all. If she waits long enough, is nice enough, and pretty enough, this mythical Prince will rescue her from growing up and, indeed, life itself, to take her off to a blissful fairyland. This Princely image becomes her god and her addiction. This is what Dowling refers to as the Cinderella Complex, the desire to be saved from adult responsibilities of life.

Just when childhood energy is at its peak, the young girl is told that she must groom herself and wait. She has been taught that her life will not truly begin until she has The Man—but there is an enormous amount of time between the introduction of this fantasy and its culmination and eventual disillusionment. During these many years we give her few acceptable avenues to allow her the *feeling* of being an adult, and even fewer avenues to the *feeling* of competency. After all, what is there to do after playing with dolls, learning to cook, mastering makeup artistry, and styling hair? In contrast, a boy has erector sets and model planes, sports, tinkering, science projects, carpentry, cars, and the like.

The curious and bountiful energy of childhood is thwarted in the young girl. She is told her place in the world is to love (men and babies) but it will be many years before she is to have this place. In the meantime, there is little else to do but wait. While she waits, she daydreams, rehearsing the fantasy, seeking idols and substitutes. She directs this tremendous pent-up energy toward kittens, horses, rock stars, Daddy, older sister's boyfriends, and anyone else who might fill the bill. It is not surprising that she has learned the art of seduction at an indecently early age, that she wants tight pants at eight and makeup at ten. After all, she probably had her place in life all figured out at five or six and there are *ten whole years* between five and fifteen. That's a lot of waiting for anyone, much less an energetic and impatient child. As she waits, her helplessness and passivity are reinforced. She learns she has little control of her life, that her life is structured by rules over which she has no influence. She becomes angry and frustrated (as we all do when kept waiting). She lashes out at her parents, usually her mother, who seems to hold the key to her imprisonment. She turns against herself, hating her imperfections, brutally comparing herself to magazine models. With reality filled with anxiety and frustration, she turns to fantasy. She spends more and more time with her fantasy lover who will someday rescue her from all this anger, frustration, and self-hate. She imagines "him" in detail over and over, his composure and tenderness, his strength and his passion. In light of this, her disappointment (if not repulsion) is understandable when she finally is old enough to date some clammy-handed, pimple-faced boy or marry a less than perfect husband.

Through her dating years, she will wait. She will wait for him to notice her and wait for him to call to ask her out. She may make some overtures, but they will be indirect and very limited. Even when a relationship or marriage has gone sour, it will usually be her place to wait for the end.

I have included a poem on waiting that I wrote many years ago.

THE WAITING

Let me now tell you of that woman
whom you have not seen before you.
It is not the strong, together, courageous,
independently individualistic woman-person
who nervously sits here performing this ageless ritual
passed on female to female

thru liberated and repressed generations—
the insane scenario of the high holy mass of waiting.
There are too many overused cliché images
of telephones that don't ring and letters that don't come
for me to begin to explain to you, a man,
this entirely feminine hell in fresh new words.
It seems as if all the women before me
have failed to make men comprehend
the double-bind straight-jacket hell of this waiting game,
then surely I would be a fool to try again.
So let me now tell you that I am waiting
thru lonely summer's nights—
you know the kind that are made for making love.
You know the kind that you simply "get over with"
thru less than mediocre sex.
I'm still waiting and believing.
Cynicism is an easy game.
Pessimism is premixed paranoia.
Independence is never needing to need.
And courage is said to be a fool's delusion.
Throughout all our realism
I wish I had been given a fairy tale or two to believe in.
I need you.
Tuck me in and tell me of better times
when you can be here to love me freely and deeply.
I will not ask for proof, I swear.
Come, please come home and release the starved child
who has spent her life
locked in a closet of sophistication and maturity.
Chase away, once more, the nightmarish phantoms
that have caused the closing of a hundred closed doors
a hundred times before I ever looked into your eyes
with hungry need and addicted distrust.
And now you have abandoned me to fight a battle
I have never been able to win.
Without a promise or a prayer
or a long-distance word of encouragement—
with only a taste of a time much more peaceful and secure
than the eternal x-ed off days that smother me by sheer number
and the traitorous knowledge that my victory
may be transformed into a defeat upon your return to me,
if you return to me.
I will wait.
I will believe.
I will believe
once more.

For many women, this sense of waiting often goes on the rest of their lives, which eventually transforms itself into procrastination and helplessness. With this continual waiting comes frustration, anger, depression, disillusionment, and grief. Though often repressed, these feelings can be almost continual and seemingly unexplained. Since this pattern is that of forfeiting responsibility, it is very common to blame others for these feelings, searching for reasons and often creating situations to attach these negative feelings to.

Women who are still caught in this waiting game continually feel restless, never satisfied with their lives and loves. They collect hurt and bitterness because they have failed to let go of the fantasy that all good girls will be rescued and somehow given a wonderful life. Because so many women have never truly released their grip on this fantasy, they have not yet begun living their own lives or facing the reality of their situation.

Women such as this carry great anger and bitterness and distrust toward the opposite sex because they have failed to live up to the fantasy and be rescuers. But this lesson is not simply learned once. Many go hypnotically through the fantasy and eventual disillusionment over and over again, still holding out hope that this time it will be different. For most of us, it takes many years and a great deal of energy and experience to let go of this cycle and move on to see men as persons, not rescuers.

Some women refuse to let go of the Prince Charming myth. Such a woman may spend her life disillusioned, discarding men or "settling for" someone who is less than her fantasy with a great deal of hurt and resentment. Having never found an adequate prince, she may decide she is an inadequate princess. Rather than live her life alone, she "settles for" a man who will become a testimony to her own inadequacy, as she attempts to remake him into a prince. Since this is not possible, eventually she will grow to pity him, be repulsed by him, or even hate him. She will also learn to hate herself as well. It is also possible that she will marry a man she truly believes is a prince, only to be disenchanted later.

The hate and self-hate, the disillusionment, the forced waiting and subsequent passivity, the seductiveness and irresponsibility of the Prince Charming myth, all lay the groundwork of depression in women's lives. This myth, in all its complexity, encourages women to forfeit their sense of personal power and seduces women into passivity. Part of what corners us into this pattern is its addictive qualities. Part of what entraps us into this pattern is fear, fear of the unknown, fear of the Boogie Man.

The Boogie Man

Scene one. She leaves her office late. On her way to her car she notices footsteps . . . someone is following her. She walks faster and finally panics, breaking into a run. The camera has become the stalker. She is cornered. She writhes and screams a moment before the ax appears. After the murder, the killer delivers a soliloquy as to why she deserved to die.

Scene two. The little girl is leaving for the first day at school. Mother nervously gathers her daughter's sweater and books. Then she begins her lecture to her child about being careful about "strangers." She vaguely elaborates about candy, bushes, and cars. The child's eyes grow wide. She understands little of what is being said, other than the fact that someone out there may want to harm her.

The Boogie Man is the masculine violence/punishment myth that is used to keep females in our culture within the strict confines of the feminine sex role. Male violence against women is a fact of life. But this is more than the acts of murder and rape. The crux of this myth is that the victim *deserved* some sort of punishment, that this violent act was justifiable retaliation for the female overstepping the boundaries of her role.

The young girl normally learns about the Boogie Man just as she is going out into the world for the first time, generally when she enters school. She is usually given very vague information as to what this "stranger" may want from her. She receives limited or no information about what she is to do if confronted with this danger. She is often told to run to a neighbor, which oftentimes just isn't possible, particularly if the molester is the neighbor.

The Boogie Man waits in dark shadows, in basements, and in attics. The Boogie Man crouches behind bushes on the way home from school. The Boogie Man lives in closets and parking lots, deserted streets, and after-hour offices. The Boogie Man lurks in the backs of cars, lonely, dark highways, and motel bathrooms. His omnipresence keeps us home, keeps us dependent and forever fearful of his retaliation, lest we stray too far, become too independent, or act too assertive. He is the culmination of our fear, guilt, and self-hate. He is the projection of our own repressed anger and disowned power.

We assume any victim somehow must have deserved his wrath. It is this assumption that is transformed into guilt which undermines our ability to protect ourselves.

Let me clarify that I do think it is important to educate children about molestation and rape. But this education must be done specifically and correctly. Those who commit rape and molestation are not usually "strangers." In fact, simply warning children about strangers may cause more potential danger, as the child may learn to be too trusting of adults who are not "strangers" and not trusting enough of strangers who might be of help in an emergency. A "what if" game is a good way to teach children to respond appropriately to a variety of potential dangers. A "what if" game, setting many possible situations, structures the discussion and allows everyone involved to relax. We also need to convey our trust in our child's good judgment and clarify that a rapist is *not* hiding behind every bush. It is important to separate the realities from fairy tales and fantasies. I can still remember believing that the reason I should be cautious of "strangers" was that they would cook me in an oven and eat me like the wicked witch in Hansel and Gretel. In the absence of real information of what a "stranger" might do to me, I had supplied the worst outcome my young mind could fathom. Let us be very aware of dealing only in the truth, lest our children become overly protected and paranoid or unduly cautious.

Everything that you can do to facilitate your child's learning to be confident in the use of her or his body will be very helpful if that child must someday face danger. Knowing you can run fast, scream loud, and kick hard is very good defense. By maintaining the belief that you are totally dependent on others for protection, you facilitate your fear and helplessness. Teach your children to protect themselves. How you go about doing this depends on the age and values of the individual. There are karate and whistles, mace and handguns to name several options. The important thing is to have some sort of defense.

By maintaining the belief that only women who somehow deserve it are raped, we symbolically distance ourselves from rape and lull ourselves into a false sense of security. This belief also facilitates guilt, the inability to protect ourselves, and just plain ignorance. It is with this same ignorance that the rapist justifies his actions.

Having dealt with the realistic version of the Boogie Man, it is important that we disarm the mythical Boogie Man. First, I suggest we remove ourselves from any media that use the kill-a-woman or rape-a-woman theme. Our minds need no more ammunition to frighten ourselves than we already have. If local news is too filled with murder and rape, then we should watch only national news. We must deal confrontively with our personal Boogie Man. We must fight our Boogie Man, prove him wrong, and not listen to his seductive paranoia. He is our own personal demon who lives off our fear and leaches our personal freedom. Starve him to death.

chapter three

American Puritanism Revisited

Our American Puritan background has strongly affected our values and perceptions regarding happiness, work, sexual mores, and life in general. These values or assumptions are so basic to our lives that we hardly recognize them. Though most of us have built our lives on these belief systems, some of them may sound so absurd that they seem laughable, while others will seem all too believable.

Despite our new-age awareness, we still perpetuate these myths with the same zealous conviction that our forefathers and foremothers did. We manage to change the jargon but the concepts remain the same. These concepts are passed on in the home, in the church, and through the media. Just as our self-image predetermines many of our limitations, our concepts about life and happiness, to a large extent, predetermine the direction we choose and the amount of happiness we allow ourselves.

Here are several of these Puritan-based myths and a brief examination of their effects on us. Some have had a stronger effect on women just as some affect certain individuals more than others. Perhaps you can add to this list.

A. *"He can, but she can't—the real message of the double standard."* The Puritans believed that women, like children, should be seen but not heard. Though we are all familiar with the sexual aspects of this myth, what we are often not cognizant of is the nonsexual aspect. This belief system relates not only to sexual acts but all action. This is the basis of all sexism in our society. It tells us that all action, achievement, and self-assertion are appropriate behaviors for men and inappropriate for women. Appropriate female behavior then becomes defined as merely supportive to male behavior. This is the underlying assumption in female fear of success and the "dropping back" syndrome of young females in the academic arena.

B. *"I must make others happy first, or I'm cheating someone if I'm happy."* Especially as females, our primary duty has been defined as making others happy. Since a woman's work is never done, there is no time or energy left to make herself happy. Vicarious pleasure is considered sufficient. Indeed, if she is happy, it is seen as a sign that she is selfishly not doing her *real work,* that of making others happy first. This paradox creates a number of very limiting lifestyles in which a woman can spend her life as a martyr, making others happy to the exclusion of her own happiness; or she can be unhappy and fail to make others happy as well; or she feels guilty when she does achieve some degree of happiness, because there are others who are not so happy.

This myth has also been carried over into economics and our values about money. We believe that we should make others rich first and that we are causing someone else's poverty if we are rich. (This will be discussed in further detail in chapter 12 on money.)

C. *"Something catastrophic will happen to me if I live my own life."* This myth is basically a punishment prophecy that tells us that if we don't live by our puritanical heritage, something terrible will happen to us. Though this country pays lip service to individuality, we value conformity much more. So we are given this myth that if we ignore the rules and establish our own life on our own terms, then something catastrophic will happen to punish us or "put us in our place."

We also attach this catastrophic punishment belief to those

who attain success. Some people were not surprised about the tragedies of the Kennedy family because the public generally believed that the Kennedy's "deserved" their fate because they were too successful (and possibly too happy).

It is this threat and resulting fear that keeps many of us from reaching our goals or fulfilling our potential.

D. *"We must earn happiness with sacrifice, hard work, and misery."* This myth can best be understood if it is divided into two sections. First, the concept that happiness must be earned is again very basic to American values. It implies that people do not deserve to be happy unless they perform in some way. This performance expectation is often linked to the impossible standards of myth B, someone else's happiness. As long as people believe they don't deserve happiness for who they are rather than who they think they should be, then people will give up on the pursuit of happiness—often before they have begun to define what makes them happy.

The second section of this myth has to do with how we are to earn this happiness. Sacrifice, again, implies making others happy instead of ourselves. Hard work tells us that happiness must never come easily, and that happiness must be a struggle. Misery tells us that happiness is earned by unhappiness. The converse is also implied—that happiness earns us unhappiness.

E. *"Work must be hard, unpleasant, and never done."* This myth has very much influenced our values regarding work and has managed to spawn millions of workaholics as well as dissatisfied but resigned workers. We learn to differentiate between work and play very early in life. We learn that work is something forced and unpleasant. Therefore, it is unlikely that it will be anything other than what we had expected. We do not teach our children that work is something enjoyable for the intrinsic value of producing something. We focus on the process much more than the product, the fact that it is a requirement much more than the creation. Consequently, it is believed that one cannot work hard enough or long enough. We also are very suspicious of anyone who seems to be enjoying his or her work. Work and play are considered opposites. He or she is seen as loafing or not taking the work seriously enough.

This myth may help in explaining the growing absenteeism, alcoholism on the job, low productivity, and shoddy workmanship that is plaguing the American economy. In China, work may not be considered fun, but it is considered valuable for its own sake—a collective creation, if you will. In contrast, some Americans see work as a daily punishment and fulfilling only for the "lucky" few who chance upon the right job.

F. *"Bad things happen only to bad people or to those who deserve it."* This is the classic myth that involves blaming the victim. It insulates us from the real world so that we can relieve our anxieties by believing the contrary as well—that, since we were good, only good things (or at least no bad things) will happen to us. This helps us believe that we can control the uncontrollable. It also causes us to feel guilty when something bad happens to us and to condemn those who have experienced misfortune.

The Puritans often tortured people for being ill, believing that the devil had taken over their bodies. Now we say that the victim must have earned some bad Karma and that he could heal himself if he really wanted to. We tend to blame a variety of other victims: The woman who is raped must have wanted it; the person who is ill is trying to get attention; the woman who is brutally beaten must have been asking for it; the person who is poor is lazy. Because of this myth, we are often overwhelmed by guilt when faced with a problem of misfortune. Consequently, we often try to ignore the problem, so we won't have to admit our badness. Most problems, when ignored, tend to get worse. So we find parents who are ignoring their child's drug problem; people who are ignoring their financial problems; and many—too many—people who are ignoring their health problems. All of them are running from the guilt that tells them that these circumstances mean they are bad and have failed in some way. All are ready and willing to punish themselves for being bad enough to have a problem rather than face it and solve the problem.

G. *"Strong women are bitches"* or *"No one will like me if I take responsibility for my own life."* Though I have already mentioned the role of the castrating bitch in an earlier chaper, this stereotype is dealt with here so that we can explore its evolution. Women who were strong-willed in the days of early America were often burned as witches. This collective female heritage combined with the Boogie-Man myth, and the very clear reality of increasing male violence against women, has taught women that they are evil if they act in their own behalf and may be punished for this transgression.

H. *"Having fun is a waste of time and sinful."* It must be remembered that our Puritan ancestors did not believe in fun. Dancing and most forms of the arts were considered sinful and tools of the Devil. Nor did they believe in relaxing or daydreaming. Today many of us are unable to relax or have fun without feeling guilty. The increasing use of alcohol and drugs may be an indication that this is the only way some people can numb their guilt enough to enjoy themselves. This myth is also partially responsible for the discontent many feel with retirement. Many of us have lost the capacity to have fun in childhood. When old age forces us to stop working, we are left with a void we are unable to fill.

This myth also makes it difficult for parents to play with their children and often forces children to an "all work and no play" lifestyle, filled with school, homework, chores, and piano lessons.

This myth also makes it difficult for people to enjoy each other as well.

I. *"There are two types of women in the world—the good girls (virgins) and the bad girls (whores)."* Before the sexual revolution of the 60s, this myth was more obviously in force. But I don't think we've come very far. Though many young females are no longer buying this myth, many young males still are. What's worse, confused by the mixed messages of our current sexual mores, many women of all ages are behaving in a sexually liberated fashion but feeling guilty and devaluing themselves.

We may be liberated enough to have female detectives on television, but those detectives are not bed hopping like the male detective shows. Female TV characters are looking sexier and talking sexier but they are not having sex and being accepted as sexual. Our culture still views sexually experienced women in the same dubious light as a used car; possibly valuable, but not as valuable as a new one (in other words, a virgin) and certainly to be distrusted.

We have a whole new breed of media virgins. The new virgins are young girls the media are selling to us as the new sex goddesses —Brooke Shields and the like. As more women become more sexually aware and active, the media turn more and more to children. We also see within this belief system that women are all or nothing, good or bad, innocent or wicked. The good girl/bad girl myth has not been eradicated from our society—it has gone underground. What we have now, in the eyes of many, are more whores and younger virgins.

I am sure there are more Puritan myths that are alive and well today in America. Many of these myths have countermyths that evolved in the 60s and have created a great deal of ambivalence and confusion. Some Puritan myths that were partially eradicated by myths before were reborn in the 60s. An example of this is the myth that is connected with myth B, which tell us it is more righteous to be poor. The Great Depression convinced many people that this was an incorrect assumption. Those people during the 40s and 50s worked very hard to accumulate wealth and protect their children from having to deal with poverty. But their children, resenting their parents' compulsive materialism, decided to buy an older and possibly more conservative myth regarding money; "It is more righteous to be poor."

So we can see that the myths remain with us as a culture. They may be transformed, guised, or in hiding for the next generation, but we don't lose them. And they have a tremendous impact on our lives.

One thing all of these myths have in common is that they are counterproductive to human happiness and often destructive. All thwart the pure human desires to seek pleasure and achieve happiness. And yet these myths hold us responsible for our own unhappiness as well as our happiness. They tell us we are deserving of pain and poverty yet undeserving of pleasure and prosperity.

Truly, the examination of these myths and their effect on our lives is very limited here and would best be dealt with as a topic of another book. They are mentioned here because of the self-limiting and destructive quality of these myths which sets the stage for and feeds depression by teaching us that there is nothing we can do to be happy that we will not be punished for. Beyond this, it teaches us that there is something good—proper, if not saintly— in being unhappy and suffering. For women, this problem is compounded. We are trained to believe that our happiness is dependent upon making others happy, we are rewarded for passivity and often punished for independent action in our own behalfs. To further complicate the problem for women, our training in passivity dependency makes it near impossible to escape the majority of these myths.

I cannot emphasize enough the importance of examining and periodically reexamining the effects these myths are having on our lives, so that we can be fully aware of the assumptions our decisions are based upon. Improving our life, by defeating depression will come only when better choices are made than we have made in the past. Better choices are made only when we can truly differentiate between our reality and the mythology of our Puritan ancestors.

chapter four

Double Messages

Through socialization women are laden with a variety of double messages, conflicting cultural "shoulds," that define how they should behave. These double messages, along with a general tendency in the culture to encourage female dependency and helplessness, provides the foundation for many of the emotional problems of women. Through the emotional double bind of these conflicting messages women learn to doubt their own perceptions of reality, distrust their emotions, degrade their feminity, and communicate in a vague, ambivalent manner. In this chapter, we will explore these lessons in self-doubt and miscommunications.

LEARNING TO BE CRAZY

Possibly the most crucial effect of helplessness on feminine psychology is that from a very early age females become dependent on others to define reality for them. Girls learn to distrust their own perceptions at the same time they are becoming cognizant enough to define these very perceptions. As a young girl becomes more and more dependent on others to define her world—to *perceive for her*—she begins to replace her reality with a fantasy that reflects the values of others. In other words, she begins to reject her reality as it is, and replace it (in her mind) with a fantasy of what the world *should be.*

Since one of the most important elements in the process of independence is the ability to separate our own reality from the reality of others (primarily our parents), it is no small wonder that this drive for independence is thwarted in females.

It is not the direct confrontation of wills between parent and child that is being discussed here. Rather it is the insidious undermining of the very perceptions of a female. To put this concept into dialogue, I am not discussing, "No, I don't want you to do that." What I am discussing is, "You don't really want to do that." Other familiar phrases that go with this concept are, "You've got to be kidding . . . you don't really mean that . . . you're exaggerating . . . you know that isn't so . . ." and the ultimate, "you're crazy."

Psychology has generally defined psychosis or being "crazy" as a break from reality. The philosophical question here that must be asked is "whose reality?" Is it my reality or the reality of those around me? If it is the reality of those around me, then which person's reality am I to choose? This is much more than a philosophical question in women's lives. Because women doubt their perceptions they become confused, depressed, dependent, and often stay in destructive situations long after any man "in his right mind" would have left.

Some women are so confused about this perceptual problem that they live with a secret terror of madness. They live in a world where they often see and feel much more than the men in their world see and feel. They know that those people who see and feel things "that aren't really there" (by definition of those in control) are labeled insane. Since women are generally more in touch with their feelings and the feelings of others than the men around them, then it follows that all women are "insane," by patriarchal standards.

Beyond the fear of madness women also experience a pervasive guilt attached to all so-called "negative" feelings. This guilt represents more than just a departure from the idea that "good girls are not supposed to feel bad" (or angry or depressed, etc.) Many women also feel guilty for what they experience whenever their feelings are a departure from a fantasy world of "goodness and light." So not only do women distrust their emotions and perceptions but they also feel guilt regarding them. They believe what they have so often been told: that they are overly sensitive, that they are creating problems that aren't really there, that they deserve these manufactured problems. In times of crisis this guilt and doubting of what are perceived as reality are a woman's worst enemies. These factors make it extremely difficult for a woman to move from reacting to a crisis and on to the problem-solving process. It also makes it difficult for her to recognize a problem for what it is to begin with.

Because of the influences of self-doubt and guilt in their lives, women often allow themselves to be easily manipulated into doing or not doing a variety of things that are against their true feelings and better judgment. The repercussions of this self-betrayal are resentment, guilt and self-hate, all of which further feed the cycle. When sexual behavior is the issue, and a woman does what she doesn't really want to do, added repercussions may be a nonorgasmic response or pregnancy.

To summarize for a moment, women are trained to doubt their perceptions and feelings. They are also encouraged to trust other people's versions of reality more than their own. When a woman's negative feelings surface or when she perceives a problem, she often experiences guilt. This guilt and self-doubt also make it difficult for her to recognize and solve problems because she doubts what is real. Because of this self-doubt and self-denial she fears her own madness, a madness built into the feminine sex role. These feelings also may cause a woman to be easily manipulated into acts (or beliefs) that are contrary to her values. When she acts against her better judgment she experiences anger, resentment, and more guilt. It is the combination of these various cycles that lets us know with unquestionable clarity that the feminine sex role, within the context of this culture, produces depression in women and predisposes women to mental illness.

CHANGING ROLES
AND THE MASCULINIZATION
OF WOMEN

Never in the history of womankind has so much been demanded of women. In the past twenty years our expectations of women have expanded dramatically, and yet our attitudes about women have changed very little. The massive introduction of women into the work force reflects the values at work here, for women have not been liberated from the responsibilities of the home but rather indoctrinated into believing that they should be able to manage the home and be a breadwinner as well.

Women have always been given double messages or mixed messages regarding what is expected of them as women. Girls are told to be good in school but not too good, to be loving and affectionate but not too affectionate, clinging, or sexual. But as sexual liberation and economics have made it permissible for women to work, now more than ever women are inundated with mixed messages from a culture that can't seem to decide what to expect of its females. We are asking women to work inside and outside the home while earning almost half of what men earn; in other words, to do twice the work, for almost half the money, while paying a tremendous emotional price.

What happens to a girl who is told that her future is limited to housewifery and then told she can be anything she wants? What happens to the psychological growth of women who have been conned into believing that sexism is nonexistent and their opportunities are unlimited when in fact sexism is rampant but well-covered? How does the Dr. Jekyll/Mr. (Ms.) Hyde straddling of old and new roles affect women? And finally, what psychological changes must women make in themselves, what emotional hurdles must they overcome, in order to compete in a world dominated by masculine values? These are some of the more important questions to be explored in this chapter.

Most women can remember the beginning of the transition in the early 60s. After all, as girls we were terribly aware of what was expected of us and terribly interested in learning to attract boys. We read all the Ann Landers and *Seventeen* magazine books that advised young ladies on how to wear their hair, what colors not to wear, and how to chase a boy without looking like you were chasing a boy. We learned how to be helpless and cute. We learned how to make him feel important and intelligent by asking unintelligent questions. Many of us grew up with Donna Reed and Lucille Ball as role models. Ultimately we fervently wanted a husband who was as good and wise as the daddy on "Father Knows Best." Those who were encouraged intellectually were aware that the purpose of their intellectual grooming was to attract and someday marry an up-and-coming young doctor or lawyer. These were in the days that if a woman went to the "best schools" it was for the purpose of catching the "best man." In the next ten years things began to change drastically. Suddenly we were being told that we didn't need to play games with men anymore (just when we had finally learned to play them so well). We were sexually liberated and the pill was there to help us with that liberation. Only through many painful lessons did we learn the bitter truth that the double standard was (and is) alive and well and thriving.

We were also given a new message regarding work. The word "career" was floating to the forefront in reference to women. Now that competitiveness, self-confidence, and motivation toward achievement had been effectively brainwashed out of us, we were told that we should have a career, not just a skill to fall back on in case some future husband died. After years of being trained to be a good catch in order to get a good catch, the tables had turned and we were being told we shouldn't waste such a fine education in being only a housewife. In another ten years we would be given the definite impression that if we were anything less than superwomen, if we had not achieved perfect marriages, with psychologically and physically well-nourished children, to be complemented by highly successful careers and well-managed efficiently-run homes, then we must be failures. Despite our feminism and our modern liberated ideals this impossible expectation seems to diffuse guilt into every dust-encrusted crevice of our lives.

Guilt is always the emotional repercussion when we are given impossible standards to live up to. Guilt, which is sometimes referred to as anger against the self, is a continual internal psychological harassment in women's lives. We feel guilty about almost everything and continually feel we are not living up to standard, because the standard itself is impossibly high and unfair. The self-esteem also eroded by this impossible standard causes great stress in the lives of women. Some women are so convinced of their lack of self-worth as compared to superwoman perfection, so tired of trying, they simply give up and slip quietly into the world of zombie-like chronic depression or drug (or alcohol) addiction.

Most women are still trying to live out both the traditional and modern (or liberated) roles of womanhood, putting on and slipping out of roles more frequently than their clothes. It is impossible to exorcize the past completely from our psyches, no matter how liberated our current beliefs are. This desire, if not obligation, to try to live out two very demanding and often conflicting roles of female behavior is responsible for so much guilt. It is reminiscent of the old saying about the futility of trying to please all of the people all of the time versus some of the people some of the time. The compulsive transformations and adaptations necessary to play the roles of the superwoman as well as the Total Woman not only produce a great deal of conflict and stress in women's lives but also produce a great deal of exhaustion as well. I am still amazed when through my private counseling work I encounter a husband who cannot understand why his wife is honestly too tired to have sex when she put in on the average of a thirteen to fifteen-hour workday between her work life and her responsibilities at home.

The conflict, emotional discomfort, and guilt produced by all this often intensifies with age. But there is a new and growing standard that provides her with an easy way out of the internal emotional battle, though this escape, like all escapes, comes with a high price. For the more a woman enters and interacts and competes in a man's world, the more she is expected to suppress her emotionality. To some extent all women experience a transition in their lives when they find themselves being put down for the very feminine traits they were encouraged to exhibit. At some point in their lives, all women will experience a conscious realization or an unconscious suspicion that the traits of emotionality, cooperation, nurturing, and sensitivity are not only undervalued in this society but considered defects or weaknesses of character. To emotionally survive this transition most women either accept their feminine nature as defective and inferior or begin a painful process of eradicating their feminine traits from their personalities and becoming more and more masculine. In a very real sense this is the hidden bargain that the masculine (but not just male) culture has made with women: They will be allowed in the business world, allowed a few hitherto strictly male privileges, provided that they are willing to forego their disturbing femininity and replace this with a masculinized personality.

This emotional metamorphosis not only happens to working women. It also is happening more and more to all women, especially to women who identify too willingly to a stoic, highly masculine husband or father. More and more young women feel compelled to hide their feelings, even from themselves, playing it tough. Could it be that the cultural answer to the problem of liberating women is to create a new woman who is a John Wayne in skirts, or an emotionally macho Playboy model?

This process of rejecting the feminine-feeling self for a more masculine nonfeeling self causes depression in women in several ways. First of all, whenever humans attempt to stop feeling, the feelings are repressed but not extinguished. Repressed feelings always cause problems, including depression, seemingly inexplainable behavior, irrational fears, alcoholism, drug abuse, resentment, stress-related physical problems, and a certain rigidity or flatness of personality.

Second, women more than men experience this rejection of feelings as a rejection of self and a disownment of sexuality. Men, after all, have been consistently raised to deny their feelings and are reinforced for this behavior. Women have spent their formative years connecting their sense of sexuality with dependency and sensitivity. Consequently, total abandonment of these values and acceptance of masculine values, which are in complete opposition to feminine values, must cause a tremendous (though possibly unconscious) emotional upheaval. Some women whom I counsel have attempted to extricate their feminine-feeling self and seem to experience a never-ending grief and diminished self-esteem because of this. It is my belief that they *are* grieving over the loss of a very real and important part of their identity.

Miscommunication

How we communicate has a tremendous impact on the courses of our lives. Because women communicate from a perspective that demands that they meet many conflicting standards, their form of communication often reflects ambivalence, confusion, and self-doubt. Most commonly this communication is indirect.

The main purpose of all forms of indirect communication is to create change or the *illusion* of change, to manipulate others without facing the conflict of taking responsibility for one's own needs. All indirect communication is based on the assumption that it is up to others to make us happy and that we are basically helpless to create change in our lives. People who communicate in this manner often see themselves as victims being persecuted by someone (or something) and hope or expect to be rescued. But all too commonly they sabotage their rescue by communicating in such a negative manner that they unconsciously manage to encourage others to ignore them, or by not communicating at all, or by communicating in such an ambivalent manner that their message is not understood.

Indirect communication tends to be either active or passive. Whining, nagging, complaining, and bitching are all *active* behaviors. Playing the role of the "mouse" or the "martyr" are examples of *passive* behaviors. A third category has to do with conflicting motives that are demonstrated through *ambivalent* behavior, such as the stereotype of the "tease."

The rest of this section on "Miscommunications" examines female stereotypic behavior that reflects active, passive, or ambivalent styles of indirect communication. Both women and men communicate indirectly and many of the stereotypes presented are certainly applicable to male behavior. My intention here is not to explore the communication problems of all people; rather, it is to look at some familiar female stereotypes in a new light of communicative styles.

ACTIVE INDIRECT
COMMUNICATION STYLES

When a woman desperately wants change in her life and is aware that some change needs to happen, she may whine, complain, nag, or bitch to facilitate that change. In such a circumstance the problem or at least the solution to the problem often involves the behavior of another person. The purpose of these active indirect communication forms is to motivate someone to change and therefore solve the problem. When the problem situation does not involve the person to whom our complainer is directing her comments, then the purpose of the communication involves several aspects. First, to elicit sympathy; second, to communicate feelings of helplessness and of frustration; and third, (and possibly most important) to give the complainer the *illusion* of confronting the problem and creating change while allowing her more easily to avoid taking any real action on her behalf. All forms of indirect communication involve repetition, particularly because other people quickly learn to "tune out" the incessant and irritating message. Whining, bitching, nagging, and complaining are all expressions of discomfort, helplessness, and *fear*—fear that she cannot eliminate her discomfort on her own *or* confront another to do it for her.

Whining involves a high-pitched vocal tone that imitates a child. Because this form of communication is so childlike others tend to ignore it, as we often do when children whine.

Bitching conveys disapproval or criticism as well as hostility. The hostility may come in a direct attack or it may involve sarcasm, but it is generally quite hostile and more direct than most other forms of active indirect communication. Bitching rarely lets an individual know what we do want, or if it does, the message is communicated in such a hostile manner that the listener stops listening in order to defend him- or herself.

Nagging sometimes does tell someone else what we want, but again does it in such a negative way that the listener does not really hear us. Nagging also does not include a time contingency. ("Will you please wash the dishes?" versus "Will you wash the dishes within the next half-hour?") This allows the listener to procrastinate. Finally, nagging is often accompanied by contradictory behavior on the part of the nagger—thereby teaching others to ignore the words altogether. A common example of this is where a woman nags her child about taking more responsibility and keeping his or her room clean, and then cleans the child's room herself, instead of delegating responsibility for it to the child.

Complaining expresses dissatisfaction over a situation but rarely lets the listener know what exactly is needed to improve the situation. It is as if the complainer is subtly saying, "If you loved me you'd be able to read my mind." The complainer often uses manipulations intended to make the listener feel guilty as a method to motivate the listener to change. It should be noted though, that many women feel guilty for complaining in and of itself. Complaining is not a negative behavior if: (1) we are complaining to the right person, i.e., the person whose behavior is directly causing us a problem or the person whose job it is to help us solve the problem (a doctor for health problems, a mechanic for automobile problems); (2) if we are clearly letting the person know exactly what changes we expect of them, (3) if we are not using guilt, hostility, or little-girl helplessness to motivate the listener. It may be helpful to think of the behaviors just outlined as "confronting," to distinguish them from the manipulative behaviors often referred to as "complaining."

It is important to recognize and confront conflict directly. We must remember that life is a process in which we must continually participate if we want to be happy. We cannot check in and out, or participate once in awhile or even halfheartedly. We are responsible totally and only for the quality of our lives. Part of the process of creating a quality life is to confront problems cleanly, directly, and as soon as possible.

PASSIVE INDIRECT COMMUNICATIONS

In women, the stereotypes of the "mouse" and the "martyr" are two good examples of passive indirect communication. Both of these styles exemplify the belief that women do not have the right to confront a problem or directly meet their needs. Both of these styles also express an internal communication problem as well as an external communication problem. In other words, because women often believe that they do not have a right to confront conflict directly or a right to meet their needs independently, they tend to passively deny themselves conscious knowledge of their frustrations and fail to communicate their needs to others.

A woman is described as a "mouse" when she is fearful of expressing her needs, frustrations, or beliefs. There is a tremendous amount of internal censoring happening in such a woman. She is very involved in what people think and is constantly comparing (at an unconscious level) her needs, desires, and beliefs to those around her. If she perceives a conflict between her values or needs and those of other people she will suppress or deny her values rather than deal with the conflict. On the surface though, she appears to have no real needs or opinions. She seems content with being a follower and caretaker of others. She is also seen as a bit boring though she is often described as a "sweet," "very nice," or "loving" person. When her bottled-up feelings of frustration surface she experiences guilt and depression, and is prone to weep. But even at this stage she will rarely express what is wrong and is often not taken seriously if she does communicate her unmet desires. Usually the bouts of depression surface more and more regularly over the years, as a result of the unique form of self-inflicted emotional deprivation that is the pattern of her life.

As compared to the "mouse," the "martyr" is more aware of her unmet needs and is unconsciously angry with those around her who lack the ability to read her mind and give her what she wants. The "mouse" believes she is not good enough to be appreciated or that she does not have the right to expect appreciation. The "martyr" believes she should be appreciated but somehow always gets passed over. Both are very self-sacrificing but where the "mouse" keeps her self-sacrifice hidden, the "martyr" finds innumerable subtle ways of letting those around her know that she is sacrificing a great deal for their well-being.

The "mouse" is depressed about other people's lack of responsiveness to her hidden needs. The "martyr" is angry about other people's lack of responsiveness to her hidden needs. Both truly believe that their needs are perfectly obvious. They also believe that love includes a mind-reading ability as well as reciprocal self-sacrifice (even if the person will feel used and resentful after the fact). In a sense, these women give much more than they feel comfortable giving or want to give, and expect others to exceed their own limits as well. It is no surprise then that these responsive styles of communication breed guilt, resentment, and avoidance behavior in those who are forced to deal consistently with women who communicate so little and yet expect so much.

AMBIVALENT INDIRECT COMMUNICATION STYLES

Some women typically communicate very ambivalently. Anyone involved in dealing with this type of communication receives a variety of double messages that in their distilled form boil down to a message of "Go away and come here" or "I don't need you and I need you." We all know people like this. This is the person whom we find impossible to understand. This is also the person with whom we never really know where we stand. One day they appear to hate us and the next day they appear to love us. This stereotype of ambivalent indirect communication represents one of the most derogatory images of women. My assumption here is not that women are the only sex that communicates in this manner. Yet women, because of their sex-role training, are predisposed to feel ambivalent about certain areas of their life (primarily love achievement and sex) and therefore are likely to communicate in an ambivalent style. My purpose in using the stereotype of the "tease" is to take one of the most grossly misunderstood characterizations of female behavior and demonstrate the problems of miscommunication that are at the root of this stereotype.

When a woman subtly communicates her ambivalence about sex she is often labeled a "tease" by the men who feel frustrated by her. Yet her ambivalence is understandable given the variety of mixed messages regarding sex that society has inflicted on her. She has been told that her main value is based on her ability to attract a man (or boy). Yet she has also been saddled with the unique responsibility of making sure that sex does not go too far too soon. This is an awesome responsibility for a girl or woman who has been socialized to be passive, nurturing, and nonconfrontive. The more emotionally involved she is with the man or boy, the more difficult a tightrope she must walk. She may desperately desire his affection and approval yet fear his sexuality. If she allows sex to consummate before some invisible deadline she may lose his affections and her own self-esteem as well as face pregnancy. This consequence looms fearfully in her mind as she dances along some mythical midline. But the consequences themselves are definitely not a myth. Studies still confirm that men/boys devalue women/girls who give sex too readily. Yet the males still feel they must press the issue, due to their own cultural sex-role training.

We can imagine these two young adults alone somewhere faced with a struggle between them, and internal struggles as well. He presses for sex as his sex-role training and biology demands; she tries to strike a compromise through some form of petting or foreplay. He is encouraged by this, assuming this is a sign of her submission. She is hoping this move will placate his desire. When she learns he is not placated but rather encouraged, she calls a halt to the whole encounter. He is angered in finding that she has regained power over a situation he thought he controlled. She is frustrated (more likely angered) by her overwhelming responsibility to conflicting values and finds him insensitive. She accuses him of only wanting sex, for there is no single derogatory term she can hurl at him that characterizes her emotions. But he has been given a name that he can use to hurt her. He calls her a "tease." He accuses her of deriving sadistic pleasure in arousing him and then rejecting him. In an effort to save face and protect his friends from her, he may use this term to describe her behavior to others.

Rarely does a woman frustrate a man for sadistic pleasure. But we all enjoy attracting and flirting. The world would be an awful place if, in the effort to be attractive, we were obligated to have sex with whoever found us attractive. But this seems to be the assumption behind the accusation of calling a woman or girl a "tease."

So, looking back over our fictional scenario we can see that the mixed messages she is communicating in this sexual situation are reflective of both the ambivalence she feels inside and the ambivalent dictums regarding sexuality that the culture as a whole has communicated to her from her early years.

There are many other situations besides those of a sexual/romantic nature in which ambivalent indirect communication may occur. For example, a woman is asked to do a favor for someone, a favor she would really rather not perform but for some reason feels compelled to do. In such a situation she may say yes, but do so with some reluctance and then proceed to act cool and aloof while performing the "favor."

In all forms, whether they be passive, active, or ambivalent, indirect communication causes communication problems, resentment and stress within relationships. These outward symptoms are merely a reflection of the internal conflict and communication problems within the individual.

Women, because of their training, are more likely than men to listen to the monologue of "shoulds" within themselves while ignoring their own needs. As women, our first task in unravelling our miscommunications with others and putting to rest the stereotypic behavior examined here must be to learn to truly listen to that inner voice that speaks to us of our own needs, desires, and values. For until we develop this ability we cannot be responsive to ourselves or others, much less behave responsibly within a relationship.

The greatest task we women have before us is to learn to trust our emotions and truly be ourselves. It is difficult to risk the loss of approval of others and give up our game of being emotional contortionists portraying some gross reflection of what we imagine others want us to be. But it is an exhausting and unrewarding game.

We must commit ourselves to be brutally honest within, to take the time to listen to our hearts without prejudging or censoring or catastrophizing. Armed with that self-knowledge we can negotiate, set limits, share, and give of ourselves to those we choose. This choice is not a compulsion, obligation, submission, or subtle bargain. Rather, this choice is communicated freely from the best of intentions and honestly offered as a reflection of internal clarity and self-love.

chapter five

Bondage

Several years ago I came across a book that fundamentally changed how I viewed the problem of helplessness versus mental health and in particular the problems of women. This book is called *Love and Addiction* and it is written by Stanton Peele with Archie Brodsky. Through this material I was able to answer a question that had been troubling me for years: Why is it that some individuals manage to work through their problems at a fairly rapid pace while others get completely bogged down with one problem and find themselves unable to get on with their lives? As I read *Love and Addiction* I began to realize that people who are unable to solve their problems may actually be *addicted* to them.

"Addiction" includes a variety of behaviors. Peele spends a great deal of time comparing drug addiction with the addiction to dependent, romantic love. In this chapter we will explore Peele's conception of dependent romantic love as an addiction and a variety of other behaviors that are frequently addictive.

Let us begin with Peele's description of addiction: "An addiction exists when a person's attachment to a sensation, an object, or another person is such as to lessen his appreciation of and ability to deal with other things in his environment and in himself, so that he has become increasingly dependent in that experience as his only source of gratification." [1]

This source of gratification serves many purposes. According to Peele an addiction: (1) structures our time, (2) provides an immediate sense of relief for anxiety, (3) distances us from the problems of the real world, (4) gives us the security of a ritual that contains a predictable outcome, and (5) gives us a sense of identity. So, addiction is a behavior that provides us with an immediate and predictable sense of relief from anxieties and escape from our "real problems." When the "high" of the experience wears off and we are faced with our "real problems" once again, the real world seems even more overwhelming than it once did. Consequently we feel even less able to deal with our problems and are more likely to perform the addictive behavior again. If we continue this pattern we will have to perform the behavior more and more often to achieve an intense enough "high" to escape anxiety. If at some point we stop this pattern we will more than likely experience some degree of withdrawal symptoms. Peele tells us that "the most intensely felt symptom of withdrawal, one that we know about only from the statements of addicts (drug) themselves, is not chemical at all. It is an agonizing sense of the absence of well-being, a sense of some terrible deficiency inside oneself." [2]

Let us look at a few examples. Consider the young woman who feels overwhelmed by the responsibility of supporting herself, who marries the first man who is willing as an escape. Their new relationship and the wedding plans provide her with an escape from her original problem. Later she busies herself with the role of "wife" in order to structure her time and relieve the still hidden issues of responsibility and meaningful work. For a while at least she has found an identity, an identity that might be quite fulfilling to one who honestly and independently chose it. But this identity can never really be fulfilling when it is concocted out of a dependent need for escape. Months or years later the effects of the escape will wear off. If childbearing and childrearing become part of the picture the eventual confrontation of the "real problem" may be postponed to midlife or even old age. But if this is the case the confrontation will be enormous, involving many other issues now attached to the same old problem. Such a woman may find herself with a husband and family she never really wanted or for which she has sacrificed too much and now feels resentful toward. She may mourn the lost years, the career it is too late to start, or even believe it is too late to find any meaningful way to spend her time. This is obviously not an uncommon scenario.

Or consider the depressed individual, whose perfectionism, feelings of worthlessness and "unlovability" make her or his time alone very painful. This person becomes a workaholic, losing feelings of self-worthlessness in compulsive work while killing any residual reminders with alcohol, television, or compulsive work at home. There are an infinite variety of problems from which people run to addiction. Some of these include problems with parents and family, sexuality, anger and assertiveness, dependency, responsibility, unresolved guilt, and problems with finding meaningful work.

There are also an infinite variety of addictions including helplessness and avoidance, approval seeking, rescuing others, fantasy, television, romantic dependent love, destructive relationships, procrastination, illness, alcohol and drugs, including caffeine, nicotine, and marijuana. This chapter looks at several of these addictions; some are covered independently in their own chapters.

First let us take a look at the addictive personality. "From interviews and Rorschach tests, some generalizations emerged. . . . They all considered hospital care wonderful, were more cooperative with staff, were more active churchgoers, and used conventional household drugs more than nonreactors. They were more anxious and more emotionally volatile, had less control over the expression of their instinctual needs and were more dependent on outside stimulation than on their own mental processes, which were not as mature as those of nonreactors. These traits yield a distinct picture of the people who respond strongly to narcotics (or placebos) in hospitals as being pliable, trusting, unsure of themselves. . . ." [3]

Another explicit portrait of the addictive personality is by Isidor Chein. "From almost his earliest days the addict has been systematically educated and trained into incompetence. Unlike others, he could not find a vocation, a career, a meaningful sustained activity around which he could, so to say, wrap his life. The addiction, however, offers the answer to even this problem of emptiness. The life of an addict constitutes a vocation . . . a vocation around which the addict can reasonably build a full life." [4]

Chein describes the addict as "pessimistic and preoccupied with the negative and dangerous aspects of life." [5] "In the ghetto setting studied by Chein, they are eventually detached from people and are capable of seeing others only as objects to be exploited. They lack confidence in themselves and are not motivated toward positive activities except when pushed by someone in a position of authority. They are passive even as they are manipulative and the need they feel most strongly is a need for predictable gratification." [6]

What is truly shocking about each of these descriptions, and the final description yet to come, is what happens when we substitute the "he" with "she." When we look at these portraits in terms of women we find not only a description of addiction but a description of femininity itself. A woman is supposed to be, is raised to be: suggestible, grateful, cooperative, religious, anxious, emotionally volatile, dependent, immature, pliable, trusting, unsure, incompetent, unable to find or untrained for a meaningful career (to some extent this is changing), preoccupied with the negative and dangerous aspects of life (cautious, afraid of the Boogie Man), occasionally able to see people as objects to be used ("womanly wiles"), lacking self-confidence and not motivated toward positive activities except when pushed by someone ("but I don't want to be a manager"), passive, manipulative, and in need of the reassurance of predictable gratification. Yes, women are raised to be addicts.

Many of the traits that our culture deems as feminine behavior and therefore reinforces in little girls predispose them to addiction. We are taught to be junkies. We are encouraged to be junkies. And we are given a variety of socially acceptable (and not so acceptable) ways to meet our addictive needs.

Chein's comment regarding the addict who has been trained to "incompetence" and lacks a career or vocation "to wrap his life around" is particularly hard-hitting and a painful reminder of the many women trained into incompetence and searching for a man to wrap their lives around. Let us look at one final analysis of the personality of the addict by Peele before we go on. I have added the words in the brackets.

The person who becomes an addict has not learned to accomplish things he [she] can regard as worthwhile [author's note: or the culture regards as worthwhile, as in motherhood] or even simply to enjoy life. Feeling incapable of engaging himself [herself] in an activity that he [she] finds meaningful, he [she] naturally turns away from any opportunities to do so. His [her] lack of self-respect causes this pessimism. A result, too, of the addict's low self-esteem is his [her] belief that he [she] cannot stand alone, that he [she] must have outside support to survive. Thus his [her] life assumes the shape of a series of dependencies, whether socially approved [such as family, school, or work] or disapproved [such as drugs, prisons, or mental institutions].[7]

Here again we see addiction, dependency, and femininity as synonymous. This may help to answer so many of the questions about the psychology of women that have baffled the experts and the general population as well. Questions like: Why is it harder for women to stop smoking or to stop eating? Why do women seem to lack motivation and the desire to achieve? Why is teenage pregnancy so prevalent in an era of sex-education and widely available birth control? Why do women stay in an abusive relationship year after year or a job they hate or a town they despise? Why do some women feel so fundamentally threatened by the movement to give women equal rights legally?

We are also left with a new and equally troubling question: Is it that the feminine sex role predisposes women to addictive behavior, or is it that the behaviors and traits which define the feminine sex role (such as helplessness, passivity, and approval seeking) are addictive in and of themselves as well? The answer to this question you may learn for yourself by the end of this next section.

A Cornucopia of Addictions

The obvious addictions involve drugs, alcohol, and food. We are all familiar with these sources of escape. We all joke about excessive television watching or workaholic behavior as addictions. These are addictions equally strong and volatile as any of the others, except they are marked with the stamp of social approval. Yet anyone who is not so inclined who has lived with a television addict or a workaholic knows the personal destructiveness these addictions can cause. I have seen many clients via my private practice who felt isolated and emotionally neglected as children because they could not compete with television for their parents' attention nor manage to communicate their problems into the time slots of the commercials. I have worked with an equal amount of clients whose parents were emotionally (and often physically) unavailable due to workaholism. These are the familiar addictions. Let's move on to the hidden addictions, those that often go unrecognized.

Approval Seeking as an Addiction

David D. Burns, M.D., in his book *Feeling Good: The New Mood Therapy,* refers to approval seeking as an addiction. All of us want and often seek others' approval. We want to be liked and loved and comforted. When someone we value gives us some form of verbal or nonverbal positive feedback we feel better about ourselves. This behavior of pleasing others began when we learned that if we acted in a certain way or did certain things we could elicit that gleam of adoration in our mother's eyes. But to approval-seek is to play-act. It is to create a performance in order to elicit the desired response. Because the act is not real, not given honestly, the response is not valid. Most children eventually realize this and abandon this form of manipulation for healthier and more productive avenues of increasing self-esteem as they learn to let go of their needs for their parents' approval.

Not all children manage to let go of this behavior, however. Some children find that they must perform some sort of approval-seeking behavior in order to receive their parents' attention. Faced with either continuing to please and placate their parents or emotional isolation, these children learn to be very good actors and actresses. So good, in fact, that they soon lose track of who they really are or what they really want. To act, to pretend, with those one loves is a dangerous game. This is especially so for a child who is pretending, creating an illusion as it were, with those who are the most influential to the developing mind of the child, those who are the makers of the child's world. The child creates the illusion of the perfect adoring daughter or son. The parents believe and respond to the illusion with love or attention. The child is not truly what she or he appears to be and the parents' love of the child is based on the illusion. The child knows this, feels guilty, and so seeks further reassurance by seeking approval behavior. The parents once again respond positively to what is essentially a lie. The most primary relationship in the child's life has become a deception. In spite of endless parental assurances the child will believe that she or he is not loved or does not truly deserve to be loved.

In adults, as in children, approval seeking is a substitute for inner feelings of self-confidence and self-love. The inner lie is that, "Maybe if I am good enough and enough other people love me I can then love myself." But of course, we never arrive at the mythical "enough."

To receive approval from others is a momentary "high" which soon wears off. Constantly seeking reassurance and more approval is exhausting and irritating to others. Because this "high" or "fix" doesn't last long we must seek another very soon or be faced with our inner feeling of worthlessness (the feeling that is common in withdrawal). Eventually approval seeking becomes a humiliating addiction. We spend more and more time doing what we don't want to do with no time left for ourselves. Resentment, anger, poor self-esteem, and depression are a few of the negative effects of approval seeking as an addiction.

Finally, it is important to note that approval seeking is a behavior reinforced in women from a very early age. We are taught to please and placate, to charm and to be helpful. Encouraged in very few areas in which we could gain some feeling of confidence, we are raised to believe that we are only as valuable as others value us.

DENIAL AND AVOIDANCE
AS ADDICTIONS

Both denial and avoidance are behaviors that often become an addictive response to dealing with conflict, whether the conflict is entirely internal or involves others as well. Denial and avoidance "get us off the hook" by allowing us to pretend the conflict never existed and momentarily avoiding the anxiety or pain the conflict evokes. When we avoid or deny conflict we will experience a short-term "high," which is basically a relief from anxiety. When the denial belief can no longer be maintained, or avoidance behavior is no longer effective, we are faced once again with the new overwhelming conflict that we have tried to run from. The mental act of denial and avoidance usually creates more fear of the conflict than one originally experienced. The more we run from something the more fearful it becomes. When faced once again with the conflict, it now seems even more dangerous (for surely it must be very dangerous if we have been running from it). If we are given a chance to avoid or deny the situation again, we will more than likely do so.

To avoid means to side-step or simply not face a conflict. To deny means to pretend the conflict does not exist. People who are addicted to these behaviors rarely get what they want or need out of life and leave many unfinished situations. They are not able to resolve or learn from conflict and develop an unreal sense of themselves in relationship to others. Often such individuals supplement this addiction with the addiction of fantasy.

FANTASY
AS AN ADDICTION

Fantasizing or daydreaming can be very pleasurable and a helpful way of distinguishing goals. But fantasizing can be very addictive and dangerous when we begin to spend too much time remaking reality in our minds. To fantasize climbing Mount Everest is healthy; to fantasize that an ailing marriage somehow will become miraculously better can be very unhealthy.

The problem with fantasy exists only when we begin to confuse what is illusion and what is real. When we get enough emotional solace from a fantasy that we lose the desire to take action to improve reality then fantasizing has taken on a negative addictive quality. Occasionally I will see a client who has replaced some unpleasant aspect of reality with a fantasy. Another person unhappy in a marriage will fantasize that everything is wonderful until the next fight. In truth, the dissatisfaction with the relationship has not dissipated nor have the basic conflicts been resolved. Rather, these individuals remade reality in their minds, busily planning for the future while escaping the anxious and painful emotional "work" necessary to get there.

Women in particular use fantasy to escape conflict and structure their time. The huge consumption of romance novels and soap operas point to the fact that many women prefer to live in fantasy, living, as it were, other people's lives rather than improving their own.

ILLNESS
AS AN ADDICTION

Illness can be addictive whether it is physical or psychological in origin. Illness often provokes feelings of helplessness in the individual and this helplessness is addictive in and of itself. Beyond helplessness, illness can be a way to control others, to achieve the attention and nurturing from others we might otherwise have to go without, and to avoid financial responsibilities (or even household responsibilities). In fact, illness is probably the best avoidance ever invented. Illness is used as a way to avoid working, success, failure, sexual contact, intimacy, all forms of responsibility, anger and disapproval from others (after all, who can get angry at a sick person?) all forms of conflict, and even rejection itself. Illness can also be a way of taking control of our lives if we feel we have been living our lives for others and lack the courage to rebel.

Revenge is also a motive for illness addiction. In this way illness is used to express anger subtly. By becoming dependent on the ones we are angry with, we force them to take care of us by failing to live up to the expectations of the persons we are angry with. Illness insulates us and gives us structure for our time, allowing us to avoid an endless variety of problems. Anyone who has had a major illness or injury knows that recovery, doctor's visits, tests, and treatments can easily use up all waking hours. For those who lack a sense of identity, illness provides the role of the "sick person." A "sick person" is not only deserving of extra love, nurturing, and attention but also not expected to provide anything in return because, after all, he or she is sick. Sick people also deserve understanding—meaning we allow them much more emotional latitude than healthy people. If they are cranky, irritable, demanding, or even irrational we must understand and forgive and certainly not get angry or confront because, after all, they are sick. Not everyone who is ill or has been ill becomes addicted to illness. Nor should someone's illness be seen as nothing more than a manipulation and addiction. But the strong social reinforcers of illness combined with the unilateral escape this vehicle can provide makes illness one of the strongest of all addictions.

RESCUING
AS AN ADDICTION

We all know people who are so busy trying to solve everyone else's problems that they never seem to notice or have time for their own. Steve Karpman calls them Rescuers. Jim Cole refers to them as The Helpers. In either case these people use the problems of others as an addictive fix to escape their own problems.

It is always easier to solve other people's problems than solve our own. It is always easier to help others than help ourselves. We all seem to know what others "should do" but are at a loss when it comes to knowing what we "should do."

Of course, there is nothing intrinsically wrong with helping others. Rescuing becomes an addiction when we find ourselves overly concerned with the lives, problems, and feelings of others and unconcerned with our own lives, problems, and feelings. Rescuing provides us with a false identity of being a wonderful, important person whom other people need. It allows us a sort of emotional one-upmanship in which we can feel we have it "all together" in contrast to these poor souls who need us so much.

People addicted to rescuing will usually complain to others about all they must do to help those they are rescuing with a tone of the exasperated martyr. But if the people they have been rescuing decide they no longer need to be rescued, the rescuers usually feel betrayed. In fact, rescuers are often betrayed, as those whom they have been rescuing eventually recognize the rescuer's somewhat pompous attitude and self-serving motive for what it is. At this point the rescuer will be either dumped or verbally attacked.

Having been trained to be nurturers and caretakers, women often become addicted to rescuing. Many mothers develop this addiction and subtly encourage their problem children to continue to have problems so that their rescuing addiction can continue. Many men, having been encouraged to be "nice guys" and to be helpful, become addicted to rescuing as well. In the end rescuers harbor a great deal of resentment toward those they have rescued. They usually feel that no one really appreciated them and often play at being the martyr. Those closest to an addicted rescuer grow to resent her or his desire to dominate others, the bossiness, the ultimate lack of compassion or acceptance of others, the generally critical nature, and the apparent lack of concern for those who do not need to be rescued.

HELPLESSNESS
AS AN ADDICTION

Martin Seligman's studies on helplessness have helped us to recognize that helplessness or submission is an easily learned response and very difficult to unlearn. A helpless response is predictable when a person or an animal is put in emotional or physical pain and given no way out of that pain. Once submission has taken place, if the person or animal is given a way out of the pain, it will not be taken. The submission is continued unless they are coerced or forced in some way to abandon the helpless behavior and act in their own behalf.

Helplessness is a highly addictive behavior. To be helpless is to fail to respond and to forfeit responsibility to someone or something outside oneself. Helplessness or passivity relieves us of the responsibility of improving our situation. In a sense, when we choose to be helpless we are saying, "There is nothing I can do." We are relieved of the anxiety of choosing to take action by telling ourselves that it is useless to take any action at all. We learn to avoid conflict or taking action for ourselves by helplessness or by not doing anything at all. As long as we remain helpless we can blame the negative aspects of our lives on others. A person who is addicted to helplessness truly believes that she or he must take life in whatever form, and that it is pointless to try to improve one's situation.

Helplessness is addictive because it relieves anxiety instantly (though temporarily), provides us with an excuse so that we do not need to initiate action, and gives us an identity of being a victim. Since helplessness breeds unresolved difficulties, the individual addicted to helplessness structures her or his time around these various sources of frustration. Rarely will such an individual actually take action to resolve these problems. Rather, this person will complain regularly to anyone who will listen. This complaining releases enough stress and accomplishes enough sympathy to enable the individual to continue the addiction to helplessness.

Helplessness is a trait very much encouraged in females from infancy. Colette Dowling in *The Cinderella Complex* points out that studies show that young mothers respond more frequently and quickly to female infants than to male infants. In countless other ways a young female is "overhelped" into helplessness. Independent action is discouraged and dependency is rewarded.

Depression is the result of helplessness as an addiction. To give up on action is to give up on oneself; depression must be the end result. Beyond depression, learned helplessness leaves individuals with a basic unresolved conflict of independence or autonomy versus dependence, a conflict familiar to all women.

The final addiction to be explored in this chapter is what I call Seeking the Endless Childhood. The addictions of procrastination and romantic love will be dealt with individually in separate chapters.

SEEKING THE ENDLESS CHILDHOOD
AS AN ADDICTION

The tendencies in females to wait, in hope or in fear, to remain helpless and to be passive, to create fantasy as opposed to dealing with reality, often culminates in a basic resistance to responsibility, if not life itself. It is as if the female psyche—in utter rebellion of finding out that life is not the sugarplum fairy world she was promised as a child—rejects life, refuses adulthood, and tenaciously holds on to her childhood by creating new dependencies.

To many women, life is a game in which they are only pretending to participate. Somewhere underneath it all, they still hope they will wake up and find it was all a bad dream, and then begin their "real life." In this "real life" we will be happy, productive, protected, loved, creative and, of course, without financial care. Caught in this syndrome, women with children imagine themselves without them. Women with even the best of husbands imagine themselves on their own.

Fluctuating between blaming, dreaming, and self-hate, many women find themselves constantly on the run. They resent everything that symbolizes adulthood and the responsibility they vehemently reject. They may play at accepting responsibility for a while, play at being the businesswoman or super mom but because these are only roles they burn out easily. They lack a sense of time and cannot imagine themselves on a continuous basis being businesswomen. They tend to overextend themselves, to take on this independent role with the same compulsiveness that they reject it. Then, feeling overwhelmed, they pull back and sink for a while in their own helplessness, fear, resentment, and self-hate.

I see a bit of this woman and this cycle in almost all women, including myself. I imagine that there are women who have worked through this major stumbling block. I imagine that there are women who get so much intrinsic enjoyment from their work and life that they have totally let go of this fantasy and subsequent resentment. There *are* joys to adulthood and being responsible. There *is* freedom, pride, and independence. Maybe this problem could be more easily alleviated if we worked on making adulthood more attractive. In the end, whether responsibility and adulthood are worth all the work is a matter of how rewarding our lives are.

Even symbols of adulthood are often repugnant to women. These symbols might include money, bills, checkbooks, being on time, budgeting, meeting deadlines, deciding on a career, exercise, school, and in general, all forms of self-discipline. Women might also see as symbols of adulthood and reject with some ambivalence their sexuality, children, and marriage. Anorexia nervosa, the disease in which women and girls starve themselves, is believed to be caused by a rejection of adulthood and sexuality. This may be the ultimate manifestation of the denial of adulthood, a rejection of food, sexuality, and life itself, with the desire to remain a child. There is a rebelliousness combined with helplessness of anorexia nervosa that I identify with. It is an attitude of a stubborn little girl who is saying, "If I can't have it *my way* then I'll take my dolls and go home . . . or hold my breath till I turn blue." It is also reminiscent of a pubescent/adolescent girl thinking, "If I can't have what I want *I'll just die.*"

The ambivalence that women feel about this independence versus dependence issue is very powerful as well as confusing and draining. We find ourselves playing "hide and seek" with our lives, taking one step toward autonomy and then fearfully taking two steps back. In the end we don't want to be stuck with being responsible and grown up. This might be a prime reason for many of those steps back after spurts of independence.

The issues of power versus helplessness and independence versus dependence may be the distillation of most of the other emotional and social problems of women. Economics, anorexia, wife beating, rape, schizophrenic thinking, and of course depression as emotional problems for women may ultimately be looked at as complex manifestations of these central issues. Not surprisingly, Stanton Peele in *Love and Addiction* tells us that this basic underlying conflict of autonomy versus dependence is the central problem for the addictive personality as well.

This concept gives us some of the first clues as to how we work with this problem. First we must recognize it as an addiction and treat it as such. We have dealt with the principles of addiction and the addictive aspects of this problem earlier. It is very important that we recognize this problem as an addiction and accept it as a lifelong problem. Reformed alcoholics know that once they have been an alcoholic the potential for alcoholism always exists. As women we live in a culture that rewards us for partaking in our addiction, so we must be especially aware of its seductive qualities.

To deal successfully with any addiction we must not be lulled into the belief that it is taken care of or overcome. We must constantly remind ourselves of its ongoing potential and our susceptibility to it. Though we must practice self-discipline we must also be forgiving of ourselves for this culturally induced "weakness" when we succumb to it from time to time. Yet it is vitally important that we do not allow ourselves to rationalize our transgressions as "not important" or punish ourselves for them either. Rather, we need to recognize them for what they are—moments of weakness or self-hate in which we indulge in our favorite (and therefore most dangerous) addiction. We are like junkies who have taken a shot of heroin or alcoholics on a binge. We will live through it; we have a hundred times before. Self-hate or remorse only compounds the problem. We have simply taken a step in the wrong direction.

How do we avoid such indulgences? First, by being in touch with our feelings, especially our so-called "negative" feelings of fear, anger, helplessness, guilt, and self-hate. If we recognize these feelings we can find constructive ways to deal with them. If we refuse to let them surface they will find their way out via our addictions.

This recognition is easiest to resolve by accepting that we *all* have a strong side and a weak side, that we *all* have aspects of ourselves that strive toward going out into the world and achieving independence as well as aspects of ourselves that pull inward and seek to have their needs met by others. There is nothing intrinsically wrong with this. If we were all totally independent and self-sufficient we would have no need to love.

Men often lean too much toward the independent side and repress the dependent side; women often lean too much toward the dependent side and repress the independent. The point here is the establishment of balance and consciousness, not repression or attempts at exorcism. These feelings are not monsters to be killed or caged, but rather to be tamed.

As in changing any behavior or tendency in ourselves, the object is to reinforce the positive, observe but not punish the negative, and keep the whole process conscious. To do this we need to make the positive behavior, namely independence, as attractive as possible and reward ourselves liberally when we act in our own behalf or persevere against our helplessness.

It is very important for women to find rewards that make independence attractive. Potential rewards may appeal to the playful, sensual child in us (i.e., fingerpaint) or may be symbolic (i.e., a new briefcase) or may represent long-range goals (i.e., a savings account for a sailboat). Posters or signs are an excellent way to keep our goals on a conscious level.

It is important that we are very patient with ourselves, that we take on our struggle one step at a time and not fall into the trap of expecting too much too soon. This is just as important as staying out of the trap of overvaluing our initial progress and thinking we are "cured" of our helpless tendencies.

Finally, we must deal in a very nurturing manner with that fearful dependent part of ourselves. Constructive nurturing ultimately fosters independence, not dependency. This means there are times that we must confront ourselves, rest and seek emotional support from others; there are also times when we must finally push ourselves forward. Most of us are not balanced as to how we "parent" ourselves. We tend to be either too demanding or too lenient. Again, the point is to balance.

In the end, growing up and being responsible can be an attractive proposition. We all remember the days when we couldn't wait to grow up, when those long years lay before us and we felt resentfully captive. There was so much to impatiently hate in those days—lack of money, lack of mobility, being told what to do and when to do it. Being grown-up seemed like the ultimate emancipation. Now we are not so sure. But like all children (emotional or physical children, that is) we bribe easily. We can reward ourselves with a new book, bribe ourselves with new outfits and promises of vacations, envision our dream houses, and pick out furniture for "someday." If you are strongly anti-materialistc I think it would be hard to make being responsible attractive, as even the self-sufficient back-to-the-land dream takes money. But such people still are bribable, it just takes different rewards.

I respond well to taking a few days off when I'm feeling overwhelmed as well as chicken soup, chocolate pudding, Fred Astaire movies, hot baths, and good cries. I am becoming more responsive to my needs, and less ego-involved in proving how independent I am. In so doing, I am becoming both softer and stronger, more emotional and yet braver and more stable. I have become convinced that if we are gentle with ourselves in our struggle toward independence, we can consistently take two steps forward with only an occasional step backward. With care, thoughtfulness, and concern, we can all become joyful and responsible adults.

chapter six

Monsters in the Closet

Depression may be experienced as an all-pervasive sense of sadness and loss, or depression may be experienced as a sense of tiredness, flatness, or a feeling of "not caring." We may feel anxious and full of fears when depressed or we may have so little energy that we believe nothing could possibly frighten us. However we experience depression, it is important to recognize that the depression itself is a cork in a bottle of many pent-up feelings and beliefs that no longer fit us. Like the head of a boil, depression covers many conflicts, many unexpressed emotions, and many frustrations. Any superficial treatment will prove futile in the long run. All too often we attempt to treat our depression superficially via drugs, ending a relationship, or moving to a new town. Such treatments may help for a time as any new stimulation or diversion may help temporarily. But eventually the trapped feelings must be exposed, explored, and resolved if the wound is to heal. Chronic depression rarely is caused by one problem or one conflict, for which there is one answer, though we all have a tendency to cling desperately to this belief. Rather, chronic depression is caused by a constellation of unresolved conflicts and unexpressed feelings. In this chapter the under-lying feelings of depression will be separated and examined to help you begin the process of psychological self-healing.

CRISES, FEAR, AND ANXIETY

Let us imagine that we are ocean explorers about to dive into uncharted waters. This dive will be a very deep one, as we search out the various feelings and conflicts hidden at different depths of our unconsciousness. Though different feelings may be at different depths depending on the individual and her past experiences and values, one emotion that is often near the surface is fear. This is the anxiety of knowing we must *do something* immediately. Since we often don't really know what the problem(s) is, we do not know what it is we need to do. This can also be as a "flight or fight" response. When an animal is faced with a threat it must either fight or flee. In the case of depression, since the threat is at best nebulous and at worst unknown, we tend to remain in that frozen moment of sheer panic, unable to make a decision or actively respond. Many of my clients have described this as feeling they are "about to go crazy." What they are experiencing is an overwhelming feeling of fear and dread that is so threatening that they believe their very sanity is being attacked.

A crisis is a problem that is so painful that we feel it must be resolved immediately. Unfortunately when we believe a problem must be resolved right away, we experience even more pain. The sense of immediacy or of impending doom makes our bodies and minds react as if we were under attack. Our adrenal glands go wild, pumping into our systems the energy to fight or run from what our minds have perceived as a very real and immediate attack. When this happens we find ourselves even more fearful. We shake, pace the floor, wring our hands, chew our nails, compulsively eat, ex-cessively talk, and find ourselves unable to sleep. We also find our-selves unable to think straight, unable to come up with acceptable solutions much less able to understand the problems that we face.

A mind that is tense, fearful, and overwrought is at its least optimal condition for problem solving. Only a calm mind can create new and workable solutions to seemingly insolvable problems. When we allow ourselves to perceive a problem as having to be solved immediately we probably will find a less than satisfactory solution, motivated primarily by escaping pain (flight) and old habits, rather than a genuine desire to find the *best* solution.

CONFLICT AND HELPLESSNESS

Another constellation of feelings that are often near the surface are feelings of conflict and helplessness. Conflict, again, refers to a feeling of being faced with a decision but in this case we are overwhelmed with our ambivalence and confusion because we believe there are only two equally unacceptable solutions to the problem. Consequently we find ourselves in a stalemate, faced with a painful problem and two equally painful solutions. This perception of our dilemma causes us to feel helpless, unable to cope with the situation, and unable to find a way out. As the helplessness sinks in, a part of us gives up. It's as if our psyche attempts to resolve this frightening and exhausting search for solutions by trying to convince us that the search is futile and we must therefore live with or accept the unacceptable.

Helplessness or giving up is like an unsuccessful suicide attempt; it is incomplete and does not provide an escape from pain. It is an illusion of an escape, as there is a great difference between release from pain and resignation to pain. Like all illusions, this illusion of not caring or having given up does not successfully recreate reality. Rather, it can serve only to protect its creator momentarily *from* reality. Such an illusion is also exhausting to maintain. When the energy fails and true exhaustion moves in, we are faced once again with a reality that is so painful that we are utterly overwhelmed. For in reality we *do* care, and a part of us is *not* able to give up, and therefore the crisis and conflict looms once again before us. This time we are even less prepared to face it than we were before. This is the addictive process that is explored in detail in chapter 5 on Bondage.

Our sense of helplessness is further perpetuated by our desire to avoid conflict at all costs. This is a common problem among women, who are often ill-prepared to deal with conflict. Most of us lack the communication skills to resolve conflict effectively. But beyond a lack of skills, women have been trained to link conflict, helplessness, and guilt in a self-defeating circular pattern, which makes avoidance almost always more appealing.

GUILT

Guilt feelings are inextricably tied to our beliefs about conflict (or subsequent helplessness). As women we do often feel guilty about (and therefore responsible for) almost everything, even though reality and our rational minds tell us otherwise. Yet we continue to pay emotional dues for those situations that we cannot control or solve, even though our minds have given up. Ultimately we must let go of our self-images as mothers/martyrs responsible for everyone's happiness, and yet continually failing to meet that responsiblity.

GRIEF AND LONELINESS

Grief and loneliness are two intense feelings associated with depression. Often these feelings are conscious. But it is not uncommon for these feelings to be buried under layers of denial. In either case, like anger, these feelings are quite deceptive. Part of chronic depression is a free-floating grief and loneliness that was formed in childhood and is being replayed in adulthood. Yet most of us fail to recognize this and attach a simpler, less threatening meaning to our grief and feelings of loneliness. We are rarely grieving *only* over what we think is the cause. Usually whatever grief or loss we experience in the present is magnified by our past experiences and thus difficult to resolve without delving into the past.

Our initial experiences with grief, loss, loneliness, and love are all formed in infancy. Infants experience all these feelings with great intensity, some more than others, depending upon the quality of nurturance received. When infants or children experience some form of parental rejection or fail to receive adequate parental nurturing, they experience profound grief and eventually exhibit signs of depression. One does not have to be abandoned on a doorstep to experience this. We must remember that the world is being perceived through a child's eyes who experiences his or her needs with an intense sense of urgency. It is difficult to tell a child "wait until later" and impossible to communicate this concept of "waiting" to an infant. When we listen to a hungry infant cry, after a few moments we often are able to detect a different tone to the crying as an infant begins to experience not just hunger but fear. This is a cry expressive of fear of abandonment, a terror of being left alone when one is completely dependent.

Maggie Scarf in *Unfinished Business* describes this as ". . . a loneliness that wouldn't be endurable: the kind of loneliness experienced by a terrified, immature child. That is, of being isolate, helpless, and abandoned, the terror of ultimate aloneness was that terror—the lost child's terror—which had to do, in the deepest ways, with fears about one's very survival." [1] This must be the primal sense of emptiness we feel with any loss, and that is the basic theme of any depression.

The sense of loss or of grieving can also be found in any of the well-accepted theories of the causes of depression. Whether the depression is caused by lack (or loss) of self-esteem, helplessness (loss of control), anger turned inward (loss of self-respect) or social oppression (loss of status), that empty, deprived feeling resonates a repetitive chord. If we lose a relationship, or a piece of ourself, the full use of part of our body, or the belief in a dream, the emotional result involves the same grieving process. We can lose a job or the security of failing (via a promotion) of our child-hood (via adolescence). We can lose our children because they grow up, or we can lose ourselves because we become too dependent in a marriage. We may lose ourselves in work or keep busy to attempt to escape this sense of grief, but with each new loss the wound is reopened.

For each of us the primary task of maturity and mental health is probably to face this aloneness by learning to nurture ourselves as opposed to searching compulsively (and regressively) for that nurturance through someone else. Maggie Scarf writes, "The capacity to be by oneself and to tolerate that aloneness well, represents a human milestone, a developmental landmark." [2] This landmark must be passed, it cannot be avoided, if we are truly to become *our selves* and be secure with the process of living.

ANGER

One traditional theory of the cause of depression refers to anger turned inward. Some experts believe that anger turned against the self is synonymous with guilt, which is also believed to be a cause of depression.

No matter what the "experts" believe, it is clear to all of us that we do not live in a culture that believes in expressing anger. Rather, anger is considered a volatile, evil emotion that should be carefully hidden. Women especially tend to believe that it is wrong (if not wicked) even to feel angry, in spite of our careful attempts to hide our emotions. Consequently, we often associate anger with guilt and try to deny that we are angry to begin with. For many of us the capacity to express anger has been punished and repressed for so long that the very idea of expressing anger is unthinkable, an overwhelming, utterly terrifying nightmare. The cultural taboos regarding the expression of anger are often reflected in the family, as Frederic F. Flach, M.D. tells us in his book, *The Secret Strength of Depression*. "There are a number of reasons why people who are chronically depressed or depression prone have a difficult time with their angry feelings. Perhaps the most important is the fact that the way in which people handle emotions is a learned pattern, passed on from generation to generation within families and cultures. If, for example, expressing legitimate anger was simply not tolerated within the home and if any show of independence or defiance was firmly thwarted, emotions would be driven underground." [3] Of course, not all families inhibit anger. In some families anger is freely expressed, especially by the males. But often even these families don't provide the best of models. In many families anger is expressed only as uncontrolled rage, a reaction to helplessness, frustration, and unresolved childhood trauma.

As women, we typically learn to express our hostility indirectly. Early in life, when we are learning that "good girls don't get angry," we develop a new set of behaviors to express hostility covertly and subtly. Such behaviors include the use of guilt ("nobody loves me"), pouting (which later progresses into depression), self-hate ("no one will ever love me because I'm a loser") and illness. These are all responses children learn to use to gain power in a situation they feel powerless in and to express anger. When these attempts are not effective, children (and adults) may escalate their manipulations to elicit a reaction from their families by hurting themselves in order to hurt others. This self-inflicted injury, as an outlet for anger, may take the form of self-depreciation, illness, or even suicide.

Why is it that repressed anger causes so many destructive problems? Because anger is first of all a constructive emotion oriented toward protecting the self. It is the emotion that lets us know when we are psychologically under attack. It is the emotion that inspires us to fight for ourselves and others. If we ignore our anger, we are in essence telling ourselves that we are not worth protecting or defending. Anger is also an action-oriented, energizing emotion that does not easily or quickly dissipate. If not discharged in some way, anger will transmute itself, becoming guilt, irritation, or depression, or collecting until the pent-up pressure erupts into violence. Of course, many people fear expressing their anger because they sense the pent-up rage within them. These people tend to be very nonassertive until they explode irrationally and sometimes violently, only to retreat in guilt and fear back into their passive cocoons.

Anger, more than any other emotion, must be released. It may demand us to take some action in our own behalfs, to equalize a relationship, to remove ourselves from a destructive situation. Sometimes, however, anger is a response to a situation that truly cannot be helped (i.e., the death of a loved one). In such a situation the anger *must still be released*. Physical discharge is always the most efficient way to release anger. The actual techniques used to discharge anger are given in detail in Chapter 9. What is important here is that the anger must be felt and vented; anger must be responded to, not ignored. The ability to respond to anger for many must be learned (or relearned) in order for the emotional deadlock of depression to be broken.

The various underlying emotions of depression are both complex and primal, powerful and elusive. Each emotion, like an individual piece of the overall puzzle of depression, must be located and expressed in order for the healing process to begin. The puzzle of depression is highly individualized, forming a personal mysterious drama based on past and present events as well as future expectations. The process of piecing together this puzzle, though often painful and difficult, is well worth the effort. By knowing what distinctive influences we are drawn to and allowing ourselves to release those old feelings that haunt us, we are free to create new lives. The process of relearning to feel all those painful hidden feelings, allowing us to let go of the past, is the process of rebirth.

chapter seven

The Black Hole

Depression, an emotional problem said to be sweeping America at near epidemic proportions, affects four to ten times more women than men. This is a very disturbing fact that cannot be ignored, and it leaves us with the obvious question of "Why?"

This chapter presents a survey of theories of the causes of depression. When compared to the previous chapters of this book, a subtle web emerges. As if society had colluded to create a depressive predisposition in females, we shall see a strong relationship between the female experience and the causes of depression.

THE FACE OF DEPRESSION

Depression can be very difficult to recognize. The emotions related to depression are so common, and the capacity to deny or cover depressive feeling is so strong (as this capacity is part of depression itself) that depression often goes unrecognized. Mood swings, anger, fear, sadness, anxiety, fatigue, changes in sleep patterns, and changes in appetite are all considered symptoms of depression. Despondency, unexplained chronic pain, inability to work or concentrate are also common in depression. Clinically, what we usually refer to as depression is actually considered "manic-depression." This fact often eludes us because many people experience only the depressive aspect of this emotional disease.

But what of the manic aspect? How do we understand this emotional duality? To understand the cyclic nature of manic-depression, we must look at grief and denial as they relate to depression.

In his studies of melancholia (an earlier term for depression), Freud noticed a similarity between the grief or mourning over the death of a loved one and depression. The three obvious differences are that, first, with depression there is a sense of deep personal failure and self-depreciation that is not evident in the grieving process. Another difference is that while grief is elicited from a specific circumstance and subsides within a reasonable amount of time (usually six months to a year), depression often arrives out of unexplained circumstances, from complex reasons, and lingers for weeks, months, years, or even a lifetime. The third difference is that in depression there is a strong desire to deny the loss or sense of loss, where in grief this denial is not evident. Depression is considered an incomplete grief, a grief held onto because the loss is not accepted. This loss, a theme throughout all forms of depression, can be the loss of a "love object" (a person one has ambivalently loved and been dependent on) or the loss of an unreal goal or even the loss of some aspect of one's self. But it is the ability to deny the loss that creates the manic cycle and keeps the depression "alive."

The manic side of depression has been described as a flight from the depressive feelings. Extreme bouts of mania include delusions of grandeur and strong excitability in which the individual is incoherent. In its milder form, mania consists of elation and a great deal of self-confidence. The individual may be witty, exuberant, and highly optimistic. A person in a manic stage of the cycle cannot relax and must compulsively keep busy. Muriel Schiffman describes the compulsive busyness as a form of denial or the repression of depression as follows:

> Busyness in the job or at home, compulsive talking, obsessive thinking, compulsive need to hear music or words continually on radio or television. Those of us who attempt to control our thoughts and feelings in order to ward off depression deliberately try to control people and events around us. . . . We wear blinders to avoid anything that might frighten us and make us experience our depression and/or the emotions underlying it.[1]

So behaviors familiar to all of us can be part of the manic aspect of depression. Just as some individuals experience only the depressive side of the manic-depressive syndrome, other individuals (though less commonly) experience only the manic aspect. At whatever frequency a manic episode is experienced, mania is an attempt to repress the emotional pain of depression. Schiffman goes on to tell us that:

> The sad thing about warding off depression is that, like most defenses, it doesn't really work. Freud said, 'The trouble with the repressed is that it won't stay repressed.' Despite all our tricks the depression is always there, just beneath the surface, contaminating all living.[2]

But how is this denial mechanism formed? Alexander Lowen (as well as other theorists) traces this capacity to the initial loss of love of a parent. In the following quote, Lowen refers to denial as naiveté.

> Most adult patients who suffer depression have not actually experienced the loss of a mother. What they did experience were disturbances and conflicts in the mother-child relationship which, however, seem to have no bearing in the patient's mind as the cause of his illness. These conflicts are so much taken for granted as being part of the normal pattern of child-rearing that the patient does not feel that he was deprived of normal mother love. . . . But the patient isn't aware of the difference between seemingly normal and healthy functioning anymore than he is aware of the connection between his illness and the events of his childhood.
>
> This lack of awareness amounts to a naiveté which characterizes the attitude of this depressed person and constitutes his predisposition of the illness. Naiveté stems from an unconscious denial of the facts of life, of one's deprivations and disappointments. The effect of the denial is to leave the individual open to similar disappointments in adult life.[3]

Later in his book, Lowen explains how the loss of the mother, or mother-love, and subsequent denial cripples the sense of emotional and physical self. This crippling leads the individual to the approval-seeking pattern that directs the life of the depressed individual. This loss of the mother's love does not necessarily mean the total rejection of the infant by the mother. Rather, all of us, to some extent, experience the loss of mother-love when we graduate from infancy to toddlerhood. An infant can do no wrong and is rarely punished except in abusive situations. An infant can be neglected, however, either physically or emotionally, or both. But normally, infancy is a state during which we can do no wrong and in which our every need is anticipated. As we leave infancy, we are suddenly faced with many limits and the word "No." We experience punishment (usually for the first time) as well as rejection when we do not conform. At the same time our dependency is often being discouraged, so in this way we also experience rejection. To some extent, we all experience the loss of the blissful infant state of mother-love. If this transition is made slowly, with reassurance and emotional responsiveness, this loss is not traumatic. If this transition is made abruptly, with little or no consideration of the feelings of the child or if the child never experiences a secure infancy, then the loss is strongly felt and often quite traumatic. It is this trauma, this loss, that sets the stage for depression, and with it a continual sense of loss.

> For an infant the loss of a mother is the loss of his world, of his self. . . .
>
> In this situation, where some part of the self is lost, the child's developing ego will strive for wholeness and completion on the mental level. To do this he must deny the loss of the mother and the self, and regard the crippled state of his bodily functioning as normal. The crippling is then compensated by the use of willpower which enables the individual to carry on, but this way of functioning is no substitute for feeling and aliveness. The denial of the loss forces the person to act so that the loss will not be acknowledged. He will therefore create the illusion that all was not lost and that the lost love could be regained if only he tried hard enough to be different.[4]

This search for lost love and self-worth continues into adulthood. As an adult, the individual seeks to "gain love and approval from the outside world and he does this by proving that he is worthy of the response he seeks." [5] Lowen says that how one seeks to prove that he/she is worthy depends on the initial values of the parent. If the parent values achievement, then the individual will strive to achieve. If the parent values helplessness, the individual will become helpful to those around her or him in order to win their love.

Beneath the apparent submission of the depressed individual to the values of the parent, there is also an angry sense of rebellion—a rebellion, Lowen tells us, that "grows more perverse with time. In most depressed patients one can uncover the attitude (generally buried deep), 'I was made to feel unwanted; now I don't really want anything.' Only by his rebellion can he mobilize the feeling that will free him to be a true person." [6] It is this attitude of emotional "sour grapes" that not only reinforces the initial feelings of helplessness, but also lays the foundation for chronic procrastination.

To review for a moment, the infant or young child experiences frustration and loss of the mother's love. The child, because she/he lacks the experience to compare to other families, assumes this deprivation or loss is normal. Rather than think the mother is not loving enough, the child assumes it is her/his own inadequacy that is eliciting this rejection. The child denies the loss by assuming it is only temporary, and seeks to regain the loss by adapting her/his behavior to prove that she/he is worthy. This unresolved conflict is carried into adult life, during which the individual will seek to undo the past by seeking approval from others. But the denial mechanism is so strong that the individual tends to ignore her/his feelings and past experiences. Her/his judgments are often poor, influenced as much by the need to prove once again that one is not worthy, as the need to regain the forever lost mother-love.

Excessive gratification of the needs of the infant can cause eventual frustration and trauma. In his book *The Courage to Live,* Doctor Ari Kiev explains:

> The most crucial period of this training occurs during initial stages of infancy. It is a time of total dependency, a time when an infant is helpless and incapable of functioning without the support of others. It is a time when either too much or too little gratification can influence adult dependent behavior.

Excessive gratification of the infant's need at this stage may foster an overly optimistic view of the world. When translated into adult behavior, this may result in an inclination to expect others to please him, and a need to make extra efforts to get them to do so. The fully gratified child has the possibility of developing into an adult who thinks the world "owes him a living." If at a later stage of infancy, when an overly gratified child gained some mastery over the world, his needs are then frustrated, feelings of abandonment may result. This may lead to a personality marked both by smug confidence and a tendency to be critical and rejecting of others.

Punishment of dependent behavior at a still later stage may lead to the persistence of the dependent behavior because it produces feelings of worthlessness and an acute sensitivity to rejection.[7]

The lost mother-love or father-love of childhood, and its subsequent quest, becomes what Lowen describes as an unreal goal in adulthood. This unreal goal is defined as "one to which an unrealistic expectation is attached." [8] It is, in a sense, a fantasy that the individual seeks which promises to undo the past by fulfilling all the unmet needs. Usually this fantasy involves the recreation of the perfect secure bliss of infancy. The adult longs for and searches for a love in which her/his every need is met while all that is expected of her/him is passive receptiveness. In such a love there is no responsibility, no fear or insecurity. Consequently, an unreal goal "necessitates an approval mode of being. In behind this goal is the need for approval." [9] The manic reaction or elation "is due to an exaggerated conceit that everything will be different this time, the way the alcoholic swears he has touched his last drop. It never is. As long as the unreal goal persists in the unconscious and directs behavior, depression is inevitable." [10]

Lowen goes on to describe the depressive reaction or depressive side of the cycle "when an illusion collapses in the face of reality. The predisposing event in the past is the loss of a love object. The loss is always the mother's love and sometimes the father's as well." [11]

This loss of love and search of an unrealistic goal spans the many specific losses that are considered the causes of depression. One can lose one's self, a loved one, one's ability to defend one's self verbally via anger, or one's feelings altogether. One can lose the sense of meaning to one's life; one can lose faith or even the will to live. Ultimately one can lose one's ability to act, to effect change; in other words, one's sense of personal power and competency. Generally a depressed individual experiences many of these losses, failing to connect this sense of loss from one situation to the other, failing to see the "theme." Women, by their prior "programming" and their very position in society, are very likely to experience these losses. Phyllis Chesler in *Women and Madness* notes that most of what women have "lost" they never really had. "Woman are in a continued state of mourning—for what they never had or had too briefly—and for what they can't have in the present, be it Prince Charming or direct worldly power." [12] Maggie Scarf in *Unfinished Business* noticed the theme of loss in the lives of all depressed women she interviewed for her very thorough and insightful book. She explained how depressed individuals create a vicious cycle for themselves via poor self-image and capacity for denial.

> What seemed to happen often was that an individual's mental set—that self-critical, self-devaluating mood—brought about unwelcome sequelae—which then served to deepen the depression, to confirm the many rotten things she already knew about herself . . . a sizable proportion [of women] who'd gotten into such a vicious negative-feedback cycle, who were constantly setting themselves up in ways that would prove once again that they already knew so well: that they were valueless individuals, worthy of little or no consideration. This is what I call the "depressive theorem." Anyone can prove it, to her own satisfaction and with the greatest of rigor, if only she patterns her life in such a way that this will happen—that her worst premises and suppositions about herself can be "objectively" supported and validated!
>
> Yet the person's own experience will be, very often, that something is happening *to* her. She will fail to make a connection between the kinds of feedback she's getting from the men she is seeing, and anything that *she herself* is doing or feeling.[13]

Ari Kiev, M.D., in *The Courage to Live,* chronicles this cycle as well.

> This constitutes a terrible, self-defeating cycle. The individual struggles to obtain the support he or she needs but never expects to receive. Uncertainty pushes the individual to test the people in his or her environment—that is, to try to *elicit* rejection to see if in

fact it exists. As a result, because of negative expectations, the individual often gets exactly what he or she expects: rejection. And the more the person focuses on the struggle, the more he or she suppresses the positive, creative aspects of the personality.[14]

Kiev remarks that this cycle is a result of "an early family situation that unreasonably both punishes and aggravates dependency." [15] There is a striking similarity between this statement and Stanton Peele's statement that addiction is caused by an unresolved childhood conflict between autonomy and dependency. Again, this conflict is at the core of all the emotional problems of women. In fact, the family situation described by Kiev is identical to cultural situations of women or girls. For in this culture women and girls are both unreasonably punished and rewarded for dependency. In describing the relationship between dependency and the behavior patterns of the depressed individual, Dr. Kiev lists five behaviors that inadvertently resemble stereotypic female behavior.

> Chronically depressed people generally are more gravely victimized by dependency than others. Their responses to frustration include the following patterns:
>
> 1. They continually seek approval and support, constantly testing the responsiveness of others, so that they are, in effect, continually "asking to be hurt."
>
> 2. They lean on others to the point where others are forced to reject them.
>
> 3. They are afraid to do independently what is likely to give them a positive sense of self because of an excessive need for approval from others.
>
> 4. They rarely experience feelings of satisfaction from their own accomplishments.
>
> 5. Occasionally they rely excessively on charm to ingratiate themselves with others. This behavior stems from an unmet need persisting from childhood to be accepted and to gain the love and approval of others. The more these needs govern your behavior, the less sure of yourself you will be, and the more prone to depression.[16]

The issue of dependency as it relates to depression is an important one. Theorists agree that the loss of love in childhood and subsequent approval-seeking lifestyle creates dependency in the individual. Such a person has not let go of the love of the parents, has not stopped seeking parental approval and therefore remains emotionally dependent, both on the parents and on those who might replace parental love. What is striking about dependence and approval seeking in women is that these behaviors are considered normal, healthy and endearing, from infancy and throughout the adult female life. This dependency quickly deteriorates into helplessness and subsequent depression. Any individual, when placed in a situation in which she or he must be dependent on another, and whose needs are frustrated, ignored, or even punished, will quickly develop helpless feelings. These feelings will translate themselves into dependent, passive, and helpless habitual behaviors which "restrict them to exactly that condition of powerlessness they most fear." [17]

Such individuals find it difficult to feel a sense of personal power or "tap inner resources, since they have shriveled through neglect. This, not surprisingly, can lead to a sense of despair and uselessness." [18]

Dr. Pamela Butler notes that these feelings of powerlessness can lead to depression in women.

> According to Martin Seligman, author of *Learned Helplessness,* when a woman experiences that she has no effect on her environment, she often develops a general feeling that what she does does not matter. If these feelings persist, depression is the usual result.[19]
>
> . . . According to Seligman, it is not so much what happens to a woman as it is her inability or her perceived inability to control what happens to her that leads to depression. And as we have seen, the traditional feminine role encourages women to surrender control of their lives to someone else.[20]

We can see a complex but predictable pattern here. First, there is dependency and helplessness, then there is rejection or frustration, then there is despair, denial, and approval seeking, which furthers the dependency and the helplessness, which increases the chances of rejection or frustration, which is met with despair, denial, and approval seeking: ad infinitum. Now let us add two more components to the picture—anger and guilt.

> According to psychoanalytic theory, the guilt and self-accusation so common among depressed patients must cover the feelings of anger and hostility toward a lost love object. Because the individual experiences guilt over feeling anger toward loved ones, and therefore has difficulty in expressing that anger, he or she internalizes and directs it toward himself or herself.[21]

This quote by Doctor Kiev explains how anger, which is a natural response to rejection or loss, is turned against the self and exchanged for guilt. This guilt is a more acceptable emotion for the dependent individual, who finds anger toward the lost love object (mother, father, lover) unacceptable. This response creates two losses out of one. Now the individual has lost not only the love object, she/he has also lost pride and self-love via the anger transformed into guilt.

An exaggerated version of the parental values becomes reflected in this guilt. The individual hopes that if she/he follows all real and parental dictates, that she/he will somehow prove worthy of the lost love.

> The depressed person is imprisoned by unconscious barriers of "shoulds" and "shouldn'ts" which isolate him, limit him, and eventually crush his spirit. Living within this prison, he spins fantasies of freedom, concocts schemes of his liberation, and dreams of a world where life will be different.[22]

Women are reared on guilt and are more likely to attack themselves with guilt than express their anger to those they love; anger is considered the most unfeminine of emotions or behaviors. So if depression is caused by anger turned against the self, as so many theorists believe, then again women are predisposed to be prime victims of depression. Now that we have established the major components of the causes of depression, let us return to this concept of loss and look at other losses that result in and are caused by depression.

THE LOSS OF LOVE:
FROM PARENTS TO ROMANCE

> The unreal goal Selma was pursuing was a relationship in which she would feel completely secure. . . . The unreal goals to which Selma had consecrated her energy were to be a perfect wife and mother, and to thereby obtain the constant and unwavering love denied her as a child.[23]

There is no area more vulnerable to the projection of the unreal goal as a means to undo the past as the area of romantic love. Though the individual with a predisposition to depression will be attracted to a variety of unreal goals, the illusion of a totally secure love will engage the energy of the individual more strongly than any other fantasy. The attraction of this fantasy is so powerful because it is truly the search for the lost parental love via the search for a mate.

> In the early transports of adult loving, moreover, some of life's earliest visions—of being fused, immersed in the being of another, of being perfectly loved, adored, cared for—are reawakened. The partner is idealized as someone flawless, a consummated, cherishing, nourishing, caressing figure (the figure of the flawless parent). The spouse will replace the imperfect parent and will be an altogether understanding, never frustrating, loving, nurturing care-giver. . . . The difficulty here is, however, that not only have one's most profound hopes of union with the opposite-sex parent been reawakened, so have one's deepest fears. . . . One knows—every adult knows—that he or she may be disappointed and betrayed in the ways that he or she was betrayed earlier. And these slumbering perceptions are, like the ecstatic anticipations of perfect love, projected or placed upon the partner. The partner becomes the mirror of one's self, and one can see in him or her the reflection of one's own greatest hopes and most desperate fears.[24]

Eventually this mirror reflects more fear than love, more disappointment than fulfillment. The fantasy dissolves, as all fantasies must.

> For the wife cannot be—nor can she become—loving peer, doting mother, and approving father, all rolled up into one perfect, caretaking being. Nor will the husband be—or become—adoring lover, cherishing father, and the facilitating, understanding, protective

mother that she has, at some unconscious level, bargained for and expected. Each one *cannot* fulfill, for the other, those needs to be parented that are so profoundly unmet. Those intense, ("childish") dependency needs become, as a consequence, mixed with intense rage and anger. The Dream of Love, which has been in large part a dream of being fully and completely nurtured, begins to develop rents and holes in its shimmering, gossamer surface—it begins to shed, to disintegrate, to fall to the earth in soiled and disagreeable tatters. And the underlying conflict, there from the beginning, emerges and grows.[25]

Scarf goes on to describe the intensity with which this loss is felt. Just as an infant in losing mother-love loses a part of herself, the dependent individual who has been searching to undo the emotional deprivation of childhood through an adult romance must also relive the painful loss of self.

The loss of cerain kinds of emotional relatedness was experienced as amputation—as the loss of valuable chunks or parts of the self. It was as if being "me" had everything to do with "being me for them" in terms of a very few, very intensely charged loving relationships. And without "them" in the picture, each woman's sense of "me" was painfully diminished . . . inevitably, for it was toward "them" that her entire existence had been oriented and upon which her own sense of self—her identity—was based.[26]

Rather than face the uncertain, when faced with the realities of adult love, many people opt out of the "love game" altogether or resentfully "settle for" a relationship that does not suit them. Either of these avenues will reinforce the depression. But through this fantasy we are given the chance to learn to let go of dependency, our childlike attachment to our parents as well as the neurotic search for approval.

LOSS OF POSITIVE REINFORCEMENT

Doctor Pamela Butler, in examining the causes of depression in her book, *Self-Assertion for Women,* points to a theory of Peter Lewinsohn, which suggests "that depression results from a lack of positive reinforcement in a person's life. Again we see that the feminine role is relevant. Because of the traditional focus on marriage, home, and children, women do not typically have as many external rewards as men. . . . In speaking of the narrow range of gratification that has traditionally been available to women, I would like to mention another reward-limiting factor women in our society face. Women are frequently treated as "nonpersons." Their actions are not recognized, not to mention rewarded. . . ." [27]

Phyllis Chesler, in *Women and Madness,* cites a study by Doctor Pauline Bart which seems to support Butler's parallel between the lack of positive reinforcement theory and the feminine sex role. In studying depression in middle-aged women, Bart "found that such women had completely accepted their 'feminine' role—and were 'depressed' because that role was no longer possible or needed." [28] The female sex role again predisposes depression by limiting the recognition and positive reinforcement that women will receive. Because the feminine sex role encourages both dependency and approval seeking, this lack of positive reinforcement is especially devastating.

> Nonrecognition means nonreinforcement, and as we have seen, nonreinforcement frequently means depression. Yet, it is typical for the feminine woman not to expect or demand recognition for her own accomplishments. [29]

So we see another cycle, consisting of dependency and the need to seek approval, followed by a deprivation of positive reinforcement (which includes lack of recognition), which leads to a depreciated self-image and, of course, depression. People ensnared in this pattern tend to wait helplessly for whatever crumbs of reinforcement or recognition that may be passed onto them, while they assume that the lack of reinforcement is proof of their unworthiness. In this way, the downward spiral continues.

LOSS OF FEELING

Depression is a "depressed" state in which the individual is cut off from her/his emotions and physical sensation. As helplessness caused by frustration takes over, the individual withdraws socially, emotionally, and even physically.

Muriel Schiffman tells us that "depression takes over when we turn ourselves off. When you stop feeling, when you screen out real emotion, depression descends like a black cloud, shutting out the vividness and intrinsic value of everything around you. Alienated, insulated from life, only muffled sounds and vague, gloomy outlines can reach you. Depression is a lonely place." [30]

If we lose our ability to feel, recognize, accept, and experience our emotions, we lose a very important aspect of ourselves. The ability to feel is even more important to survival than the ability to see, speak, or hear. Lowen suggests that "the suppression of feeling creates a predisposition to depression, since it prevents the individual from relying on his feelings as a guide to behavior. His emotions do not flow in sufficient strength to give him a clear direction, that is, he lacks what it takes to be an inner-directed person. He loses faith in himself and is forced to look to the outside world for guidance." [31] The suppression of feeling contributes to both the capacity for denial and the further development of dependency.

When the ability to feel is repressed, so is the ability for self-expression. This perpetuates the isolation of the depressed individual.

> In the depressed individual self-expression is severely limited if not entirely blocked. In many people it is limited to a small area of their lives, generally their work or business, and even in this defined area, self-expression is limited if the person works compulsively or mechanically. [32]

Ultimately, the loss of feeling and self-expression results in a loss of aliveness. This causes the continued sense of mourning that has been associated with other losses mentioned earlier in this chapter.

> Depression is a form of dying, emotionally and psychologically. The depressed person not only has lost his zest for life, but has temporarily lost the will to live. He has, to the degree of his depression, given up on life, which is why depression is so often accompanied by suicidal thoughts, feelings, or actions. [33]

The loss of one's sense of aliveness makes it difficult to find the energy to go on, while the reasons for living and meaning of one's life slips away.

TIMING

Maggie Scarf's theory on timing cannot be overlooked if we are to have a complete view of the causes of depression. Scarf draws together the factors of timing, coincidence, and frequency of stressful situations to help us better understand why depression hits some individuals and overlooks others in similar circumstances and from similar backgrounds.

> Another important factor that can't be left out here is the matter of timing. Whether or not one contracts an illness—be it flu, depression, or some other disease—has to do not only with "exposure," but with one's state of functioning at the time that it happens. . . . The impact that a particular environmental insult— a loss, an injury, a separation, a trauma of any variety—has upon a particular individual, depends not only on the force or degree of the stress (that is, the virulence of the flu germs), but upon that person's own state of being at the time that the stressful life experience is encountered.[34]

Timing is crucial in understanding the causes of depression. This vulnerability determined not only by the past but also by the unique circumstances of one's life, helps us to understand how stress makes us more vulnerable to depression.

Finally, here is some very helpful and profound advice provided by Muriel Schiffman. "You must unlearn the destructive lesson taught to us all our lives, which was: ignore depression, pull yourself together, keep a stiff upper lip. *Pay attention to depression.*" [35]

PART TWO

chapter eight

Nurturing Ourselves

So far this book has focused primarily on the problems of depression and the sacrifice of personal power, looking specifically at the causes of these problems in women's lives. Now it is time to shift gears and begin to look at some very tangible ways to overcome these problems.

To solve any problem, we must begin with accepting responsibility for the problem. This means that beyond recognizing the problem as well as its source, we must commit ourselves to solving the problem without reservation. It is not enough to know that the problem exists or how the problem developed. We must translate that knowledge into constructive and consistent action. But to overcome the problem of depression and reclaim personal power, we must be willing to let go of a variety of attitudes regarding emotional problems and happiness. It is in this way that we can let go of our view of ourselves as the "victims."

One such attitude mentioned by Wayne Dyer in *Pulling Your Own Strings* involves the belief that we are victims of past experiences and training. Obviously the premise of this book is that our past experiences and training very much influence our present attitudes and behavior. However, our past does not control us; we are helpless victims of our past only if we choose to be.

We need to look critically at the past and to determine what emotional handicaps we have brought into the present. Each of us has had some negative experiences that have limited our abilities to make ourselves happy. No one has managed to emerge from childhood totally unscathed. Each of us received training that proved harmful and experiences that were painful. Though the past provides us with important information, it is pointless to bemoan our past, using it as an excuse for our present situation. If we are aware enough to know how our past is affecting our present behavior, then we are aware enough to let go of the past and move on to changing our present and our future.

A similar belief that many of us maintain is that there is nothing we can do to change ourselves. We may even tell others, "This is just the way I am. I can't help it." This is, of course, an excuse we make to ourselves and others in order to escape responsibility for our behavior, while the truth is that all of us can do a great deal about our behavior and our feelings.

Another belief we must confront and free ourselves of is that if we avoid thinking about our problems they will somehow disappear or at least not bother us as much. This rationalization is motivated by the desire to avoid conflict with ourselves and others. It is this desire to avoid conflict that has entrapped us into the role of the "victim" to begin with. When we lose the desire to confront and resolve conflict and permit ourselves to be seduced by avoidance, then we have essentially forfeited control over our own lives.

The belief that others control our ability to be happy also creates a situation in which we will be victimized by others and victimize ourselves as well. Though the actions of others will often influence our feelings, we have a great deal of latitude as to how we choose to perceive these actions. If we base our sense of happiness on the behavior of others, then we have made a tremendous investment in controlling others, which is, in the long run, a very risky proposition.

The concept that no one can really *make* you happy or unhappy is often difficult to grasp. When we are unhappy, we blame others or even a particular situation for our unhappiness. All too often those moments of bliss we strive for are the recreation of situations when we have won the approval of others in the past.

Let us say, for example, that you have a co-worker who is a very negative person. When you get to the office she never has a kind word, but all too often offers a sarcastic comment. She complains throughout the day and manages to make the work environment less congenial. You have a choice as to how you perceive this individual. If you perceive her as someone who should change, who should be positive, you will surely be disappointed. If you seek approval from this person, (who rarely gives her approval to anyone) or if you let her behavior determine how good or bad your day at work will be, then you are essentially using this person to make yourself unhappy.

It is simply self-destructive to base our sense of security or happiness on anyone else's behavior other than our own. People are basically predictable, but it is equally self-destructive either to assume people will change or that they will not. No matter how much people talk about changing their behavior, they have not changed until they have changed. In other words, it would be silly to change our conception of others *before* their actions have proved our former view of them is no longer valid. However, sometimes people do change and not always for the best. So it is important that we do not invest too much of our sense of security in anyone else's behavior.

Beyond the possibility of the people whom we are close to changing, situations change as well. Here again we have the opportunity to see the changes in life as either negative or positive opportunities. Again, the choice is ours.

Finally, there are a few myths about mental health and illness that must be dealt with. First is the belief that only crazy people feel emotional pain or have emotional problems. This belief is dealt with in detail in the chapter on "Handling Emotions," but let me stress now that pain and problems are part of the human condition. Many believe we must be able to feel pain and face problems in order to feel joy and peace. All of us have moments of deep despair or pain in which we may question our sanity. But, to a certain extent, our capacity to feel pain and admit we have problems is more a symptom of sanity than mental illness. Another myth regarding mental illness is that only weak or "crazy" people need help with their emotional problems. Humans, however, are very social animals, which means that, by nature, we were not meant to "make it" on our own. This belief stems from a very computer-like masculine attitude that sees all displays of emotion as neurotic and the desire to be comforted as weak. This attitude is very destructive to one's mental health. Humans naturally need the support and comfort of their own kind in times of difficulty. To need and seek help for emotional problems is not sick, weak, or neurotic. To deny having emotional problems at all, to expect one should always be able to handle them on one's own, to see those who reach out as weak or crazy is, in fact, a neurotic attitude that causes much emotional pain, deprivation, and isolation.

The last attitude about mental health and illness that must be challenged is the belief that if one works hard enough at one's problems (i.e., takes enough workshops, goes to enough therapy, reads enough psychology books) that someday we will arrive at a mythical point of being "together" when all problems and painful feelings will disappear forever. Generally the longer we consciously work on our problems the less frequently we will be in pain and the fewer problems we will create for ourselves. But as long as we are alive we will face some pain, some conflict, some problems. We can learn to roll with the punches better, duck more quickly, and even punch back more effectively, but life is never consistently lacking conflict or pain. For these things, as well as an infinite variety of other feelings and experiences, "come with the territory."

All the attitudes and beliefs just covered help entrap us into behavior that allows us to be victimized by others and encourages us to use others to victimize ourselves. Why would we want to be victimized? To avoid taking responsibility for our own lives. For many individuals the predictable pain of victimization is more acceptable than facing the unpredictable unknown as well as the responsibility of our own happiness.

In letting go of these "victimizing beliefs" we must replace these attitudes and behaviors with something new. This brings us to the concept of "nurturing" ourselves. To nurture ourselves is to be responsible for and responsive to ourselves. To nurture ourselves is to nourish ourselves—to provide sustenance, to cause growth, and to provide training. We must learn to raise ourselves as loving, concerned parents would raise us. It is our obligation just as it is a parent's obligation to give more to ourselves than the pure necessities. We have a responsibility to encourage ourselves to be responsive to our emotions, to provide direction for ourselves, and to search for reliable people to help us meet our needs. Just as a good, nurturing parent would attempt to compensate for the negative early experiences of an adopted child, we must now adopt ourselves, providing ourselves those experiences that we have so desperately missed. Responsible adulthood should make up for or compensate the negative experiences of childhood, providing a balance.

All of us missed some crucial positive aspects of nurturing in childhood. Maybe we did not receive enough physical affection from our parents. In that case, we must be sure to break this pattern by surrounding ourselves with genuinely affectionate friends. Possibly we were never encouraged to face conflict and solve problems. If so, it is important that we gently but firmly encourage ourselves to face conflict. A good parent listens, responds, comforts, confronts, encourages, sometimes forces, and often rewards. It is this sort of parent that we must be to ourselves.

Most of us have long abandoned the child within us. We ignore this child's needs, giving it only the barest of necessities. Yet this child's needs occasionally become overwhelming. When this happens, the child in us tends to meet its needs in childlike and familiar ways—ways that in an adult life are often inappropriate, if not self-destructive. We must teach the child within us new and better ways to meet its needs so that this child can grow into a responsive and balanced adult. By nurturing ourselves, we can wean ourselves of addictive patterns, heal ourselves of old trauma, overcome emotional handicaps, and reclaim our personal power. By nurturing ourselves we can learn to accept and love ourselves, while helping ourselves to become even more of whom we want to be.

Some Practical Suggestions on Nurturing Yourself

1. Become aware of the negative messages you internally tell yourself (i.e., "I'm stupid," "I'm afraid," or "I can't do anything right"). Then create positive statements that are the opposite of these negative statements (i.e., "I'm smart," "I'm relaxed and confident," "I am doing everything right"). These positive statements are called

affirmations. Use them frequently. Tell them to yourself in the morning while bathing, while driving in your car, while eating your lunch, and before going to sleep. They may feel like a lie at first, but keep on using them. Affirmations are one of the most powerful self-help tools available today, so use them frequently.

2. Develop a healthy curiosity about your personality and your behavior. When your behavior seems inappropriate, question yourself and don't be satisfied with simple excuses. Learn to dig into yourself, searching for clues or pieces of the puzzle. Ask yourself often, "What am I feeling?" "What does this remind me of?" "What am I really upset about?" "What was happening *before* I began to feel this way?" Take knowing yourself more thoroughly as a project.

3. Learn to be responsive to your needs. When you feel down or frightened, ask yourself the way you might ask a child, "What can I do to help or make me feel better?" If your biological child was down or frightened you wouldn't reprimand her/him or ignore her/him. Become a *good,* responsive, nurturing parent to yourself.

4. Often we feel ambivalent about a situation, as if we had two equally strong parts of ourselves that felt completely opposite about the same situation. When this happens, use Gestalt therapy to help resolve these two opposing forces. In Gestalt therapy you will use two chairs. In one chair you are on one side of yourself. In the other chair you are the other side of yourself. Using the two chairs you will begin a dialogue, a conversation between these two sides. Speak from one side of yourself in one chair and, when you feel it's time, change to the other chair and reply. Continue this, listening carefully to what evolves. (Use a tape recorder if you can.) This process always feels stiff and silly at first. But push yourself to continue and you will learn a great deal about yourself. This technique is also helpful in resolving past conflicts with others or conflicts that are taking place in the present. In this case, use one chair to be "you" and another chair to be the other person. Respond as you might imagine the other person would respond. For more on this technique, read *Gestalt Self Therapy* by Muriel Schiffman.

chapter nine

Handling Emotions

Most schools of therapy have in common two basic beliefs regarding emotions. First, the emotions need to be expressed or expelled. Secondly, the repression, or nonexpression of emotions causes most forms of mental illness, neurosis, and psychic (and often physical) pain. The term "getting in touch with one's emotions" has become the battle cry of the human potential and psychological growth movement. But this battle cry, this therapeutic process of relearning to feel, has met a cool response on the part of the American public. Why? Because in this culture emotions are still associated with weakness or uncontrolled violence. The virtue of self-control is held far higher in the eyes of the American public than any definition of mental health. We still tend to associate courage with the ability to hide emotions rather than the ability to express emotions. Somewhere beyond all the therapies and soap operas, beyond our cultural lust for violence and drama, Star Trek's "Mr. Spock" (an emotionless man) is the American people's real hero.

It is fitting then that the psychological world sees its primary task as teaching the American people to recognize, feel, and express (in appropriate ways) the whole gamut of human emotions. For emotions, as much as our logical perceptual mind, keep us in touch with reality, and therefore sane.

Emotions, when recognized and dealt with, serve us in many ways. Generally, emotions add depth and color to our lives. They move life from a flat, black-and-white, two-dimensional place to a three-dimensional, technicolor sphere. Emotions give meaning to our lives, allowing us to love, create, feel contentment, and peace. Emotions allow us to feel all those uncomfortable feelings as well, such as worthlessness, rejection, jealousy, and hate. Emotions help us know when we are behaving congruently with our values or moving toward our growth. Emotions help us make complex decisions about intangible situations so that we can solve problems and arrive at solutions that fit our needs. When we ignore our emotions it is as if we have chosen to ignore what we have seen or heard. Whenever we betray ourselves in such a fashion, we inevitably pay a heavy price.

Each specific emotion serves a purpose. Again, to ignore an emotion because it is unpleasant would be like ignoring the tactile sense of pain when touching a hot object simply because the feeling was not comfortable. In this chapter we will briefly explore the world of emotions. As we examine several emotions one by one, we will focus on their purposes, their meanings, and some constructive methods to deal with the more unpleasant emotions.

Emotions must be dealt with. We must deal with many things we cannot see, i.e., pain, government, responsibility, even many forms of illness. Because we cannot see these things makes them no less real or important. To move away from emotions, to repress or ignore them, is like choosing to perform a lobotomy on ourselves and is, in fact, psychological suicide. We can be happy, fulfilled, and growing only when we pay attention to and respond to the message of our emotions. This is as it should be, because our feelings are the guiding force of our lives.

A NOTE ON
BEING TOO EMOTIONAL

Somewhere along the way many of us have been told that we were being "too emotional." One of the reasons we hide our emotions is to avoid this accusation. There are two points to be clarified here. First, we cannot truly be too emotional; we can, however, express emotions in inappropriate ways, or make a decision based purely on emotion. Second, when someone accuses us of being too emotional she or he is almost always attempting to manipulate us by making us feel weak or crazy. The real message behind the manipulation is "I don't like the emotions you are expressing" or "you are causing me to feel emotions I am afraid of."

A SMORGASBORD
OF EMOTIONS

Pride

This is a good place to start because pride is a feeling of worthiness or a feeling of elation regarding an achievement, accomplishment, or possession. Pride is a positive affirmation and a belief in our own goodness. However, pride all too often is confused with conceit, which is defined as too high an opinion of one's abilities or worth . . . "too high" meaning unrealistic with a definite tone of looking down on others. Because we want to avoid conceit we often avoid pride as well. This confusion has cost us the satisfaction of appreciating who we are and the thrill of doing our best. The next time we do something well, which doesn't mean perfectly, let's boast a little. When we face a fear, get a promotion, or handle a sticky situation better than usual, give ourselves a pat on the back. By rewarding ourselves along the way we will continue to grow into the kind of persons we want to be.

Exercises
for Developing Pride
1. Make a list of all the things you are reasonably good at. Include all hobbies, personality traits, and skills that you consider assets. Make this list into a poster that is a positive description of "you."

2. Celebrate any achievement on your part. Go out to dinner, buy yourself a present, ask a friend to join in the celebration. (Remember that an achievement is any new accomplishment, i.e., facing a fear, losing five pounds, being assertive, etc.)

3. An outward manifestation of pride is being able to ask for what you want from others and to refuse to be used, abused, or manipulated. Assertiveness is an act of pride and self-love.

4. You have an opportunity every day to experience pride by managing your time well and rewarding yourself for getting things done. Conquering procrastination will help you achieve a sense of pride.

5. Daily you also have the opportunity to risk being a little more of whom you want to be. Each day you are faced with the possibility of being friendlier, more honest, and more assertive. To be the person you want to be, to live your potential fully involves many small actions (rather than large changes) on a day-to-day basis, all of which will increase your feelings of pride.

Apathy

Apathy is defined as a lack of emotion or feeling, or a lack of interest in things, or a feeling of indifference. This is often a feeling of "not caring" or of mild boredom. Apathy is common in depression and signals us that for some reason our lives lack meaning.

Apathy is also a signal that we have lost touch with what makes us happy. Life has become merely an exercise in killing time.

Helplessness coexists with apathy. Apathy always involves a sense of having given up, which is also common to the feeling of helplessness.

Grief consistently lies just below apathy. Apathy may tell us that we "just don't care" but ultimately this is a rationalization to protect ourselves from the pain of grief. The state of apathy or not caring must always elicit some form of grief, because in choosing apathy, in choosing to "not care," we have betrayed ourselves. By giving up on our abilities to make our lives better, we have lost our best friend and defender—the self. With this loss must come a sense of grief; whether it is conscious or not is another matter.

Apathy is a dangerous emotion. It is an emotion through which we gain distance from ourselves, our motivation, even our sense of self-preservation. Therefore, if left unchecked, it will grow, until we lack any reason for creating a better life or even living at all.

Exercises
for Reducing Apathy

1. The child in you can help you find the way back to your feelings. Do things that might appeal to your inner child. Try baking cookies, coloring, playing with modeling clay, or going on a swing. Give yourself time to rediscover fun.

2. Use your fantasies to tap into your values and potential. Each day tell yourself a story about a totally different life you could have. Be an adventurer, a pirate, a city executive, a country doctor, a world traveler. Use your imagination to rekindle your appetite for living.

3. Create a daily schedule for yourself that includes rest, rewards, fun, exercise, social contact, and work. Make yourself follow the schedule, ignoring the whining child in you that complains, "I don't *want* to."

4. Exercise and being with nature are two of the most effective ways to "wake up" your life. Use them.

5. Find someone who needs your help, to give your own life meaning.

6. Do the exercises on grief and helplessness.

7. Extend yourself socially. Meet new people and reestablish old friendships.

8. If mornings are hard, eat breakfast out with a friend or watch one of the morning shows on television. Add a morning walk to get yourself going right.

9. Apathy is a good reason to consider counseling, especially if you are feeling so apathetic that you can't seem to do any of the above suggestions. Apathy should not be ignored. It is a dangerous emotion and indicates a need to take immediate action.

Helplessness and Fear

To feel helpless is to feel impotent, weak, powerless, and unable to take control of our lives or effect change. When we feel helpless we see ourselves trapped and often experience alternately both the panic and submission of a trapped animal. Helplessness is different from apathy in that the pain of the conflict is more surfaced. There is a sense of giving up and yet a desire to regain control. Because of this pain and desire the giving up is not complete. With apathy, at least on the conscious level, the giving up and submission are complete. With helplessness the message is, "There is nothing I can do about it" ("it" being some conflict causing psychological pain). With apathy the message is, "I don't care" . . . which is a logical progression from the ongoing pain of helplessness.

Helplessness has all the potential dangers of apathy. As mentioned previously, it is a highly addictive emotion, giving us a sense of relief from anxiety when we tell ourselves that we cannot take action because there are no acceptable solutions. Helplessness tends to expand into our lives and become a growing, malignant, self-fulfilling prophecy. The longer we allow ourselves to feel helpless, the more we become immobilized and the harder it is to take action. It is easy to move from feeling helpless to becoming helpless. Helplessness, like a forest fire, tends to spread from one area of our lives to another, because when we fail to take action we begin to doubt our *ability* to take action in general.

The opposite of feeling helpless and fearful is to feel powerful. Power is another word that has negative connotations, especially for women, who have been trained to see virtue in weakness. For many of us, "to feel powerful" means to dominate or to control with aggression. To clarify though, one dictionary defines power as "the ability or capacity to act or perform effectively." With this definition it becomes clear that working toward increasing our capacity to feel powerful is synonymous with increasing our abilities to lead successful and fulfilling lives.

Exercises for Developing Personal Power and Decreasing Feelings of Helplessness

1. Overcoming helplessness and instilling a sense of power in your life can be achieved by consciously defining what you need and creatively finding ways to meet those needs.
2. Assertiveness training will increase your sense of power and overcome feelings of helplessness.
3. Using anger constructively will help increase feelings of power. Anger is a wonderful tool to combat helplessness. Try getting angry at the helpless part of you that whines, "I can't."
4. Learn karate, aikido, or another form of self-defense.
5. Learn carpentry. Hammering, working with power tools, seeing the fruits of your labor is a wonderful way to get in touch with your power.
6. Reclaim your immediate environment by moving the furniture

around or moving to a new place altogether that better suits
your needs.

7. Camp or backpack by yourself or with an equally inexperienced
   friend in a wilderness area.

8. The more control you exercise over your life, the more you define
   what you want out of life and work to meet those goals, the more
   courageous you will feel.

9. Overcoming helplessness means you must challenge conflict rather
   than avoid conflict. This means you must learn to face the anxiety
   and uncertainty, and learn that all conflict offers the opportunity
   for becoming more powerful.

10. Fear is very much a part of helplessness. Though fear can exist with-
    out helplessness, helplessness *cannot* exist without fear. You
    can reduce helplessness by reducing fear. The simple task
    of recognizing and expressing fear will greatly reduce its power.
    In doing this it is very important that you separate the feeling
    (fear) from the decision-making process. All too often fear
    governs decision making, so that the underlying motive of all
    actions is to escape fear. When this happens you stop growing
    because all your actions and decisions are safe and familiar, based
    on doing that which is the least anxiety provoking.

Fear must be challenged to be reduced. We have a tendency to
embellish a few facts with a great deal of catastrophizing.

Sharing our fears with someone who will give us moral support without discounting our fears often helps reduce their impact
as well. Even a simple statement to ourselves such as "Right now,
I'm afraid" will help a great deal. Breathing deeply and fully will
reduce fear as well. Try breaking down that task or fear that is
producing anxiety to many small tasks. This is what I call "toe-
dipping." First you stick your big toe in, then your whole foot, then
your leg, etc. Be sure to reward yourself along the way.

Guilt

Guilt is anger turned against the self. For most of us it is more than
simply taking blame for some wrongdoing. It is a punishment of
emotional self-abuse as well.

To borrow from Transactional Analysis a moment, guilt can
be thought of as an abusive parent battering a child. Guilt does not
listen to intellectualization or reason. Being a bully, guilt understands only one thing, anger.

We must defend ourselves from guilt. It is a destructive, depreciating emotion that beats us raw and leaves us exhausted and vulnerable. The tiredness associated with depression is often a result of the constant abuse of guilt. If we do not defend ourselves from the guilt, we begin to believe its incessant tirades and begin to act out its awful predictions. Guilt lays traps for us and waits patiently until we fail, ready to spring on us with full force. We cannot escape guilt. No amount of drugs or alcohol will slay it, but rather these attempts at escape only feed it more venom.

Guilt can be controlled and dissipated. It cannot be killed but it can be caged and partially tamed. To do this we must face our own personal guilt monster with all the anger and pride and courage we can muster.

I am not going to suggest a variety of exercises to cope with guilt. Rather, let me give you one specific step-by-step process to confront and control guilt.

1. Have your guilt write a letter to you. Be as brutally truthful as possible. Let your guilt, in written form, have its say.
2. Take a few days to be aware of your guilt. Record how many minutes and hours you spend berating yourself. Listen to your guilt in all its forms, from its quiet whispering, to its loud accusations. Become aware of its most frequent messages. Write them down for later use.
3. Write a letter to your guilt. Let your guilt know how you feel about it. Let it know that you are no longer going to let it control you.
4. Draw a picture of your guilt. This may end up being some evil distortion of one of your parents or it may resemble you or even an animal. This is not a lesson in art. If you are too self-critical to let yourself draw your guilt, then do an impressionistic drawing of of how your guilt feels.
5. Create a series of affirmations to counteract the messages of your guilt. Use them regularly and consistently.
6. Create a single line that characterizes your willingness to fight your guilt. Examples might include "Shut up," "Get off my back" or various combinations of four-letter words. Use this statement of defiance whenever you are aware of your guilt berating you.
7. Now imagine your guilt is your pillow. Talk to it, yell at it, and punch it repeatedly. Let it know that you won't be dominated

and abused any longer. Fight back with all your strength and anger. Defend yourself and keep punching until you can't punch anymore, until you are absolutely exhausted. Then, and only then, stop and relax, breathing deeply. Use your affirmations. Repeat as often as necessary.

Finally, remember if you do not fight your guilt, you will begin to believe its message. Because guilt is basically misplaced anger, it must be expelled as must all forms of anger.

If you do not fight your guilt then you have betrayed yourself in your unwillingness to defend yourself—the ultimate price of which is always depression.

Anger

Anger is often disguised as irritability, resentment, jealousy, depression, or apathy. Though anger is often seen as a destructive, violent emotion, it can be a very positive emotion if it is dealt with in a timely and constructive manner. The message of anger is always an alarm letting us know we are being threatened and that there is a need for self-defense. Anger helps us overcome the fear of taking action in our own behalf. Anger becomes destructive and/or needlessly violent only when we ignore its message too long and/or we do not exercise conscious choice over how we defend ourselves.

Let's look at the example of the young mother who finds herself getting very angry with her three-year-old who has been very disagreeable all day. Her anger builds from early morning on and it is not an easy day for either mother or child. Each confrontation the mother carefully checks her anger which is therefore not dissipated and so it accumulates. By the end of the day the mother is exhausted and potentially explosive. The message of her anger is essentially, "This kid is driving me nuts and ruining my day." Her anger is in response to the control the child is exerting over her life. The child is also acting as a threat to the mother's stability and happiness. If the mother recognizes this early in the day she could find many ways to regain control over her life and respond to the child's needs. She might take the child to the park, where she could relax a bit and the child could play. She might leave the child with a sitter or a friend for a couple of hours and go home to take a hot bath. Or she (and even the child) could get involved in some activity that demands heavy physical exercise to discharge some excess energy. This last suggestion is very important as all anger needs some form of outlet. To deal properly with anger we must recognize and respond to it promptly, find a constructive way to defend our needs, and physically discharge the anger.

It is very important that we recognize the anger as early as possible. Anger is like an emotional smoke alarm warning us of danger. A smoke alarm is nothing but an irritating noise if we ignore it. So is anger draining, distracting, and irritating if it is not responded to promptly. How many times do we not say something we should say, not respond assertively by defending our emotional needs, only to irrationally explode later, and remorsefully punish ourselves with guilt? When we do not respond appropriately to our anger, our anger will always find an inappropriate release in retaliation to our nonresponsiveness, directed either at others or at ourselves. Repressed anger directed toward others takes many forms, including sarcasm, irritability and defensiveness, projection (accusing others of being angry with us), resentment, or passive aggression (slamming doors, being late, "forgetting" to do a promised task, etc.). Repressed anger not directed toward others becomes directed toward ourselves in the form of guilt, depression, fear, and a variety of physical complaints including various forms of pain (especially neck and back pain), stomach and intestinal problems (including ulcers), tiredness, and lack of sexual desire. Ultimately, anger, when repressed, ruins our relationships, our bodies, and our lives.

After recognizing our anger we need to determine its message. To do this we must ask ourselves, "What part of myself do I feel is being threatened or is under attack?" We might also ask ourselves, "What must I do in order to protect or defend myself?" Sometimes we will find it impossible to answer these questions until we have taken the next step of physically discharging the anger. If this is the case then we must postpone this problem-solving step and take care of discharging the anger first.

There will be other circumstances when we will know the answers to these questions. Often in these situations taking appropriate action will physically discharge the anger as well. The goal is to give the anger a harmless outlet so that none of it will remain to plague us. Anger is a very potent form of energy, and all energy is basically positive. If energy is repressed and not given a constructive (or at least harmless) outlet, then it will become destructive energy. Usually anger can be discharged only by some form of physical action. These actions could include repeatedly punching a pillow, lying on one's stomach and beating and kicking a mattress, repeatedly hitting a pillow with a tennis racket, playing racketball or hardball, hoeing a garden, yelling, screaming or roaring like a lion, and running. Women have used housework for centuries as a way to dissipate anger but I doubt housework would do the job completely, with the possible exception of beating a rug over a clothesline with a broom (which is rarely done anymore).

It is vitally important that all forms of physical discharge are done consciously (while focusing on the anger) and to the point of exhaustion. If they are not done to the point of exhaustion, if we stop out of boredom, cynicism, or tears, we will be left frustrated and irritable. Some forms of physical discharge are fairly quiet. Some can be done around others and seem perfectly normal, such as going for a run or a very fast walk. In any case, there is nothing wrong with saying, "Excuse me, I'm a little upset right now and need to get this out of my system." People usually understand and respect this sort of honesty.

Physically discharging anger will not increase the likelihood of becoming violent with others. In physically discharging the anger we are greatly reducing the potential for violent action against others.

Finally, we must learn to make friends with our anger. When we yell, punch a pillow, or actually defend ourselves we are clearly in touch with our power. It is a statement of our innate value and worth and respect rather than fearing our anger. In our willingness and ability to defend ourselves we are saying, "I am worthy of being treated fairly and I will not tolerate being abused." This is an act of self-love, which teaches others how we want to be treated. We must learn to own our anger and take pride in our ability to defend ourselves. In so doing, we will learn the power of self-respect.

Lust and Love

Lust is a feeling of intense sexual desire. It is meant to be a joyful emotion but is sometimes a problem when it is either taken too seriously or repressed. To be in touch with our sexual feelings is a beautiful thing. It makes us feel vibrantly alive and attractive. But lust does not mean that we should necessarily do anything about the attraction or desire, or that we are in love.

Often we do not allow ourselves to feel lust because we consider it unsafe or bad. This repression happens only when we believe we are not in control of our sexuality or that we should always act on feelings of lust. Feeling sexual is a wonderful feeling just to allow ourselves. No action is necessary. We *choose* to act, but we may also just quietly and privately enjoy the feeling of being in touch with our sexuality.

Because women have been led to believe that they are bad if they are sexual, they have often confused lust with love. As a young adolescent I was unable to distinguish between these two emotions, which led to many compromising situations.

Love is an emotion that takes time to cultivate. Respect, mutuality, and common experiences are necessary to form a loving feeling.

Love is confused with lust in another way as well. Many people feel they should be sexual with any person of the opposite sex (or sometimes even the same sex) that they feel love for. This fallacy causes many problems. It forces some people to feel obligated to have sex when they would be better off being loving friends. It also forces some people to have friends only of the same sex as themselves and never really to get to know the opposite sex as friends. It also inhibits same-sex friendships because of the fear that loving feelings, if expressed, will be misconstrued as sexual feelings.

Once again, lust is not love and love is not lust. Certainly these feelings can coexist, but these feelings can exist independently as well. Love is more than a feeling of intense liking or sexual desire. Love is an experience built over time. Lust is an intense sexual high. By learning to differentiate and enjoy both lust and love, we will have a better, more fulfilling relationship with ourselves and others.

Grief

Grief is a feeling of deep sadness in response to a loss. The loss may be clearly evident as in the loss of a relationship, the death of a spouse, or the loss of a job. Or the loss may be more subtle, such as the loss of a dream, the loss of physical health, or the loss of self-image. In the last few years, because of the interest in the subject of death and dying, there also has been a good deal of literature written on the process of grieving.

It is natural for humans to experience a number of different feelings over a fairly prolonged period of time after a loss. Generally, after a loss we experience a period of disbelief, shock, or numbness. After this disbelief wears off we experience intense mourning, often along with anger. Day-to-day functioning is difficult and we may find ourselves unable to remember simple things and become highly disorganized. Later there comes a need for us to find some sort of meaning for the loss. We may be able to see ways in which we may possibly benefit from the loss. We may decide that the loss will make us stronger or free us to face some issue we had avoided in the past. As we work through our struggle with meaning, the pain of the loss is reduced and we are able to integrate the experience.

These stages may not be experienced singularly. We may feel grief and anger simultaneously, and our struggle for meaning may come early in the process as well. It is also possible to become fixated (stuck) in one of these stages, which prevents us from completing the grieving process and letting go of the loss. This is common when a child experiences a loss of a parent (or a parent's attention) and consoles herself by saying "I don't care." When this happens the child becomes fixated at the stage of disbelief and is therefore unable to express her feelings of sadness and anger, or resolve the loss.

Grieving is ultimately a process of cleansing and healing. Like all processes it cannot be rushed. It can only be nurtured and trusted. To heal fully we must give ourselves to this process. We must allow ourselves to cry and trust that the tears will eventually stop. We must allow ourselves to feel these bitter feelings of anger and resentment as we wonder in anguish, "Why me?" We must give ourselves the time to mourn without accusing ourselves of feeling sorry for ourselves. We must give serious thought to the meaning of this loss without condemning ourselves with guilt. In the end, when dealing with loss, however blatant or subtle, we must treat ourselves gently, patiently, and lovingly. When we do this the final result of our efforts, our work, and our pain will always be the seed of growth . . . a new beginning.

An exercise in unfinished grief. Sometimes the grief is old and unfinished. Sometimes the grief is over a subtle loss, an aspect of yourself that you are letting go of. In either case, make your loss more real by having your own funeral. Funerals are rituals of grieving, loss, and letting go. Write a letter to that which you have lost. Write about your feelings. Be as detailed as possible. Allow yourself to cry for as long as you need to. Then burn your letter, saying whatever prayer or meaningful words that seem appropriate. For the next few days or weeks allow yourself to be "in mourning." Wear dark colors or some memento that reminds you of your loss. Spend some time talking with a friend or writing on the meaning of this loss. Be quiet and especially kind with yourself. You will know when your mourning is over and you are ready to go on to a new, richer life.

Boredom

Boredom is an emotion that lets us know that we are long overdue for change. Usually, when we are very bored with an aspect of our lives, the boredom spreads to other aspects of our lives as well. Boredom lets us know that it is time to take some risks.

If we are truly honest and willing to be courageous enough to be responsible, then we are never bored. Life offers continual change and a variety of opportunities, if we are willing to trust in ourselves and risk change. But many of us have been raised to believe that change is bad and that security is in keeping things the same. This is a risky approach to life that makes death the ultimate goal, because only in death are we guaranteed "sameness." Real security comes from the ability to welcome change. To welcome change, to seek change, comes from the natural growth-oriented desire to improve ourselves continually and our circumstances. The answer to boredom is risk, movement, and growth.

If we do not seek change and stay with the false safety of boredom we risk becoming rigid and depressed. To fail to move toward growth is an act of self-betrayal. It is also a risky delusion, for change ultimately comes, and if we have an emotional investment in keeping things the same, we will be unable to deal with or make the best of the change.

I find it helpful to think of life as the ocean, forever changing. Those who learn to swim in the ocean accept its movement and learn to predict its movement so that they can pass through a wave effortlessly. Those who cannot accept the movement are crashed on the shore and left sputtering, scraped, and frightened. Finally there are those who learn to become part of the ocean, who can use its waves to propel themselves (surfing) for the sheer joy and excitement of becoming something larger than themselves.

To continue with this analogy, boredom is synonymous with those on the beach who never risk learning how to dive through a wave. They stand on the shore and longingly watch the surfers. Occasionally a wave may catch them off guard and crash into them. They may love the ocean and find it beautiful but they will never become part of it because their fear is greater than their desire to be something more.

It is clearly not possible to cover all emotions within one chapter of one book. I have tried to cover the more troublesome and confusing of emotions. Needless to say such emotions of peace, joy, and playfulness are equally important. An absence of these emotions has a message as well. It is vitally important that we involve ourselves in activities that provide us these very positive and important feelings.

The direction of our lives must be toward experiencing positive, self-enhancing feelings more and more often. The paradox is that we must often allow ourselves to experience the unpleasant emotions of fear, anger, and grief in order to experience the pleasant emotions more frequently. The prescription for growth—for realizing more and more of our potential—is to feel, respond to, and integrate this new information.

Emotions are at least half of our being, and certainly the more exciting half. We must dare to feel. We must trust what we feel. If we do, we will learn the meaning of who we are and who we were meant to be.

chapter ten

How to Get Going

IMPROVING SELF-CONFIDENCE

Women have notoriously poor self-esteem. This is reflected in every aspect of female existence. Women hate their bodies, underestimate their abilities, and tend to avoid challenges.

In dealing with the problems of helplessness and depression, we must remember that there is a definite relationship between positive action and feeling better about ourselves. When we lose this connection we feel stuck and trapped. We imagine that we will take positive action when we feel together. Actually this rationale is backward. We must take positive action in order to feel better.

When our self-esteem has waned, we have simply stopped acting in our own behalf and given in to helplessness and self-hate. We punish ourselves for real or imagined wrongdoing by boycotting our self-interests. We stop, we withhold, we' fantasize and berate ourselves. We punish ourselves for inaction by further inaction as our self-esteem deteriorates even more.

To break out of this cycle we must begin to treat ourselves

with respect and to act with self-respect. The actions we have so long withheld from ourselves tend to take several forms. These are assertiveness, problem solving, and time management, which includes goal-setting and ending procrastination. All these behaviors are skills that can be learned with practice and persistence. These skills produce movement, change, and self-respect in our lives. These skills also tend to reduce chaos in our lives and help us to deal with problems early and effectively. These skills provide our vehicle to happiness and are crucial to developing self-esteem and overcoming depression. But we must be willing to risk in order to learn any new skill or achieve anything worthwhile. We must be willing to risk disapproval of others and the loss of the security of the known reality if we are to create a better life for ourselves and achieve self-respect. A risk, yes. But well worth it.

Some Practical Suggestions
for Improving Self-Confidence and Self-Esteem

1. Work on developing skills and areas of competency. This means challenging yourself to learn new things continually. Learn to grow house plants, play a musical instrument, speak a second language, cook a gourmet meal, play bridge, ski, be a manager . . . the possibilities are limitless, so don't limit yourself.

2. Learn better social skills and force yourself out into the world to meet more people. Remember that they are as frightened as you are, and try to focus on making them more comfortable. Social skills and social self-confidence are learned only through practice, so get out there and practice! A course from your local community college on interpersonal communications may help. Of course, be sure to reward yourself for each new excursion in risk.

3. Write a list of your fears, focusing especially on activities you would like to do but fear has held you back. Pick the easiest one and slowly face it, using small steps at a time, rewarding yourself along the way. If you would like to go back to school, start with going to a speech or event, then talking with a school counselor, then taking one fun and easy class, slowly working toward your goal.

4. Wean yourself from letting others (or manipulating others to) solve your problems. If you feel you really need advice, research all the possible solutions, collect them, ask everyone, read books on the subject, and then armed with lots of possibilities choose one that fits *you*. Or better yet, combine several of the alternatives to create a plan of action that is both comprehensive and tailored to meet your needs. Allow yourself the exhilaration of facing on your own a problem that you have traditionally asked for help with. Then reward yourself for your independent action.

5. Set achievable goals for yourself in a variety of areas. Think of your life as a pie. There are a number of pieces in that pie, including relationships, intimacy, spirituality, work, play, hobbies and activities, environment (home life), community, physical and mental health. Set easily achievable goals for yourself in each area you think could use some improvement. Break each goal into smaller steps and add a time or a date to each step. Make a poster to remind yourself of your direction and be sure to reward yourself along the way.

6. Remember that each crisis provides us the opportunity to develop ourselves and become more self-confident.

7. Write a list of things you have been dependent on others to provide. Take one at a time and find other ways to meet those needs. This does not have to be permanent. It is a lesson in knowing you always have other options, which is a key to independent behavior.

8. Give up all nonpositive ("not bad", "bad," or "not good") relationships no matter how much they need you, if at all possible. Work on replacing these nonfulfilling relationships with better ones.

9. Learn to take time to yourself, for yourself, to enjoy being alone, doing things you enjoy. Take a walk, drive to a new place, go to a movie, take a bubble bath. Learn to give of yourself, to yourself, because you are worth your time, your attentions and your love.

10. Give some honest thought to the needs of those in your life whose relationships you cherish. Instead of passively responding to their requests, find active ways in which you can show them how much you care.

11. There is nothing that will improve poor self-image and weak self-confidence faster than a new external image. Change your hair style, try new makeup, buy new clothes, or get a friend to help you put together new outfits out of your current wardrobe. Create a new you!

ASSERTIVENESS

Studies have repeatedly shown that women typically communicate in such a way that undermines their believability. Even more importantly, women all too often refrain from communication directly, hinting at rather than simply stating their desires.

If we do not communicate clearly our needs, wants, opinions, and desires, or if we communicate in such a self-effacing, placating manner that our message can be easily disregarded, than it is impossible to control the course of our lives or maintain self-esteem. Assertiveness is a skill that teaches individuals to communicate directly, clearly, and with conviction so that they will be understood, believed, and respected.

Assertiveness is literally a survival skill in this highly complicated, crowded, and competitive society. The more busy and full our lives become, the more we need to hold our own and effectively deal with conflict. To regain control over our lives, to regain lost personal power, we must learn to behave and communicate assertively. Assertively is not aggressively, it is not abusing others. It is expressing ourselves in a way that is direct and in such a way that communicates self-respect without "putting down" others. If we wait with our hands out for someone else to give us what we want and deserve out of life, we will be deeply disappointed. To have what we want out of life, we must learn to act and communicate in our own behalf, because we deserve to have the kind of lives we have always wanted.

The purpose of this chapter is to give you the philosophy of assertion. But there is another equally important part of assertion that cannot be taught in any book. That is the "language of assertion;" in other words, learning to use vocal tone, inflection, and words in such a way as to make your message sound congruent (so that the message sounds like the meaning of the content) and effective or powerful. This sort of assertion must be learned in a live classroom or workshop situation. You should be able to find a class or workshop on assertiveness near you, either through an educational institution or through a private therapist.

There are many reasons why we are not assertive. The most basic reason has to do with the training we received as children. Most of us were labeled "good" when we were cooperative, passive, and willing to forfeit our own needs and desires for the benefit of others. We were labeled "bad" when we were unwilling to forfeit our desires, when we were uncooperative, aggressive, or demanding. Since the primary way in which we were punished for so-called "bad" behavior was through the use of guilt, we often feel guilty as adults when we are assertive. When we feel guilty, we chastise ourselves in the way that our parents once did. We tell ourselves that we are bad, selfish, and "not nice." We remind ourselves that no one will like us (or love us) if we continue to behave so badly. We often truly believe that if we put our needs first and act in our own behalf that we are failing those we love.

Let's take a moment to examine this concept. Are we really being selfish when we act in our own behalf, when we assertively express our needs, opinions, and desires? Are we somehow cheating others by choosing to take care of ourselves first? What are we taking from others if we accept the responsibility of creating our own happiness?

It has been said many times, in many ways, that we cannot truly give to others if we cannot give to ourselves. Expecting others to make us happy is an enormous responsibility to require of them. It is incorrect to assume that if we take care of our own needs, we will be taking something from someone else. Self-sacrifice as a pattern of behavior or compulsion is not an honest form of giving because there is almost always a hidden bargain involved. When we sacrifice our own needs for the needs of others we expect something in return. Since the bargain is hidden, it is basically a deception and rarely is fulfilled. This causes resentment. Resentment is an anger that kills loving feelings quite effectively. When we habitually sacrifice our needs for others the ultimate outcome is always a damaged relationship. Certainly from time to time in all relationships concessions must be made and compromises created. The question here is whether occasionally to make sacrifices or compromises or whether habitually to put our needs second to the needs of others. When we compulsively sacrifice our needs for others we are making a statement that others are always more important than ourselves. In a very real sense we are using others to put ourselves down without their consent. This act is a bastardization of love. We are not taking anything from anyone by expressing our opinions, taking responsibility for our own happiness, or standing up for ourselves. Rather, by being assertive we are giving others the gift of our true selves.

Another reason people are not assertive has to do with lack of knowledge or skill. Many people, especially women, simply don't know how to be assertive. The option never occurs to them that they can be assertive. The words never come to their minds except as an occasional afterthought.

When lack of skill is the issue, people refrain from being assertive because they lack the communication skills. Such individuals try to express themselves but fail to do so assertively. They may refrain from being asssertive too long and then express themselves aggressively, along with a great deal of pent-up hostility. Or they may express themselves in such an apologetic, self-effacing manner that they are not taken seriously by others. Because of their lack of skills, these individuals rarely achieve their desired results and give up on assertive communication altogether.

Often, anxiety and fear block the ability to communicate assertively. Fear can paralyze the ability to communicate honestly. The fear and anxiety involved usually has to do with concerns over rejection or violence. We fear that if we are assertive others will hate us or label us "mean," "ungrateful," or "bitchy." We imagine that if we are assertive we will lose our jobs or destroy our marriages. Justifiably or not, we often fear that assertiveness will elicit a violent response.

Finally, people often talk themselves out of being assertive. Dr. Pamela Butler in *Self-Assertion for Women* refers to this as "negative self-talk." [1] We may tell ourselves it is not that important. We may tell ourselves our ideas or feelings are not valid when they conflict with others. The list of things we tell ourselves is near endless. This is a very destructive brand of self-inflicted brainwashing that disrupts our ability to be truthful with ourselves or others.

Assertive Behaviors

Here is a list of assertive behaviors to help you get a better sense of the true nature of assertive communication. Assertive behaviors include but are not limited to: (1) direct eye contact, (2) proper inflection, vocal tone, and volume, (3) assertive physical placement in a room, (4) assertive stance or posture, (5) assertive clothes (yes, you can dress to command respect or be ignored), (6) initiation of conversation, (7) negotiation, (8) stating preferences, (9) requesting help, (10) stating limits, (11) refusing, (12) expressing positive feelings and compliments, (13) accepting compliments, (14) expressing anger and sadness, (15) initiating physical affection, (16) confronting constructively, (17) dealing with manipulation effectively. This list will help you evaluate how assertive you already are and in which areas you need to improve. To improve you must practice, risk, evaluate the results, and try again. Only in this way will the anxiety of trying something new dissipate and assertiveness become a natural, comfortable way to communicate.

CONFRONTATION

There are many occasions when it is necessary to confront others. Sometimes the confrontation is quite spontaneous because the behavior in question is unexpected (i.e., someone talking loudly in a movie). Other times the behavior has taken place over a period of time and so the confrontation is planned. Either way, any confrontation needs to include these four elements: (1) our feelings (which we should admit to rather than accuse others of causing), (2) an objective, specific description of the behavior that is bothering us, (3) suggested alternative behavior, (4) finally, we need to give the person we are confronting an idea of how the proposed behavior change will improve our relationship.

This formula is an adaptation of a confrontive script outline by Mary Bolten, an assertiveness trainer in the Sacramento area. Each confrontation may demand a change in the formula. We may want to begin with our feelings, or the behavior we want, or the behavior we want changed. Each person, each confrontation demands an adaptation dependent on personalities, power relationships, and timing. The more practice we have at confrontation, the more our experience and intuition will help us find the best adaptation for the situation.

Some Practical Suggestions

1. Keep an ongoing tally (in your mind or on paper) of each time you say yes to something you really don't want to do. Continue this exercise for two weeks.

2. Write a "Declaration of Independence." This statement should include how you expect to be treated by others, your responsibilities and limitations in helping others, your expectations to be in control of your life and happiness, etc. Make this statement into a poster and place it somewhere where you will see it often.

3. Practice "sounding believable" with a tape recorder. Try sentences like, "I want you to be quiet," or "Please go away, you are bothering me," or "No, I don't want to." Say each sentence *very slowly,* and be careful to articulate each word clearly. Often women speed up the last few words or raise their inflection at the end, which makes the statement sound like a question. Experiment with sounding pleading, angry, unsure, and firm. Try each sentence and then play it back, critically listening to yourself.

4. Find a friend to role play with you a confrontation that you need to have or have had (but unsuccessfully). Practice your best and worst fantasies of what might happen.

5. With the same friend, have a mock fight. Yell at each other. Call each other names. Learn to desensitize yourself to anger.

6. Practice positive assertion by giving compliments and initiating conversations. Smile at an elderly person in the streets, talk to a child, compliment a co-worker on a new haircut, and let your spouse know how much you appreciate that small favor. Assertion is the gift of yourself that can improve not only your life but the lives of others as well.

Problem Solving

When faced with a personal problem, few people actually think about the problem-solving process. We tend to react emotionally and then reach for the quickest and easiest solution, which is rarely the best solution.

How we feel about a problem is important, but all too often our feelings paralyze us into inaction, until we are overwhelmed with panic and then react, as opposed to problem solving and then taking action.

Problem solving is a thinking process in which we form a creative response that not only eliminates the problem but also improves the situation in such a way as to meet personal goals. Problem solving is based on the belief that we have the right and responsibility to create a better life for ourselves and solve our problems in such a way as to be responsive to our own needs, desires, and goals. In *The Universal Traveler,* Don Koberg and Jim Bagnall define problems as "situations that need improvement." [2] A truly assertive growing individual, who is working toward growth and the fulfillment of potential, sees problems as an opportunity to face conflict, question old assumptions and choices, and create out of chaos a better life. A problem-solver not only creatively solves problems but also is more than willing to recognize and even create problems. This is what Koberg and Bagnall refer to as "constructive discontent." [3]

The following is a distillation of the formula for problem solving presented in *The Universal Traveler.* Through teaching problem solving and my own personal experiences, I have found this process to be extremely useful in handling all sorts of personal problems, no matter how large or small.

First, the problem must be accepted. This is easier said than done, as all too often the biggest obstacle in preventing the solving of a problem is the nonacceptance of a problem. To accept a problem means to completely accept the problem situation as it currently is. We must be willing to let go of any fantasies that the problem doesn't really exist or will somehow spontaneously resolve itself. To accept the problem we must commit ourselves wholeheartedly to solving the problem. Often it is only later in the problem-solving process that we find we have not truly accepted the problem.

The second stage of the problem-solving process is to analyze the problem. We must compile all our feelings, all the facts, everything we know about the problem. This is best to do in written form. It is often helpful to keep a list of questions as we work through the analysis stage.

Next comes the definition stage. With definition the object is to state what we do want out of the situation. Acceptance and analysis express what we have. Definition expresses what we want, our goals or needs. It is often at this stage that we find what we thought was our problem is not really the problem at hand but rather another problem altogether. If this is the case we must go back and begin the process again. The best way to work toward a definition is to list goals in order of priority and then make this list into a brief paragraph. Now pretend for a moment we are taking out an ad that will cost us $20 per word. Work on deleting as many words as possible from the paragraph without losing any of the essential concepts. Try to develop the briefest statement possible. Another helpful exercise involves making a list of the subproblems related to the problem and then prioritizing these problems. When this is done it often is the case that what we thought was a subproblem is the "true" problem.

Koberg and Bagnall tell us, "When forced with a problem situation don't do the natural thing and ask, 'what can I do?' . . . instead ask, 'what is the true problem of this situation?' " [4] Once we have defined a goal the fun begins. The next step is to brainstorm as many possible ways of reaching that goal *without* judging whether these ideas would work, would be distasteful, would be moral, etc. That's it . . . absolutely no judgments. The object here is quantity, not quality. Do get as bizarre, silly, and creative as possible. When you think you have run out of ideas, spend an evening with a friend and see how many suggestions the two of you can come up with. Ask another friend and possibly a stranger as well. Again, remember we are going for quantity here, not quality or practicality. Put a dot next to the ideas that are appealing.

The next exercise involves making a list of all the negative and positive aspects of each idea with a dot next to it. After we prepare this list it is a fairly simple task to create an overall plan of action that includes the best aspects of each idea. A good comprehensive plan involves many actions and the best of the ideas. Each action should then be divided into subactions or small steps. For instance, if part of the plan involves going back to school, action would include contacting the school, sending transcripts, meeting with a school counselor regarding choice of classes, registering, etc. After all the actions are broken down into small steps it is very important to add time contingencies to each small step. A time contingency is a specific date or time of day. This will help us make a commitment to our problem-solving program and help us not to procrastinate. The final part of this program development phase is to add a reward to each date on our plan. A reward at the end is not enough. We all need encouragement along the way.

Finally it is time to begin to act in the program. It is important to evaluate along the way, though it is equally important *not* to overvalue initial progress lest we forget to follow through on the rest of the program. Oftentimes the plan must be modified a bit along the way. At some point it is apparent that the plan has either worked or has not worked. If the plan has worked it is time to move on to another situation that needs improvement. If the plan has not worked, it must be evaluated to determine what did not work and why. It is often helpful to go through the whole problem-solving process again, beginning with acceptance to check, to see if the right problem is being worked on.

Problem solving involves a good deal of work and forethought. Oftentimes we must struggle with our resistance toward expending the energy necessary to find the best possible solution. Many of us are basically lazy about solving problems. We want an easy, quick, painless answer. But such an answer is almost always the wrong answer, that perpetuates rather than resolves the problem situation. Consequently it is important that we practice and become familiar with the problem-solving process. Eventually it will became like second nature and most of the process will happen unconsciously. We will find ourselves less and less dependent on the written word as we become more comfortable and creative with the problem-solving process. As this process becomes more and more a part

of us, our attitudes toward problems will change. We will find ourselves viewing problems as opportunities for growth. Each problem
will present another challenge to play a creative game that enables
us to construct the lives that we truly desire and deserve.

Controlling Your Time
By Ending Procrastination

What are we avoiding? What is it that we know we need to do for
ourselves, but we just can't seem to find the time to do? Controlling
our time means taking control of our lives. The first thing we
must face about time management is that we often don't truly
want the extra time. We want to paint but somehow can never
find the time amidst all the demands made on us. We want to
find a better job, but who has the energy to job-hunt after a
long day of work? There are many good books on time management with programs for organization and nifty lists. But in the
final analysis, the difference between those who always seem to
have enough hours in a day to do everything they want to do, and
those who can never find the time to do anything they want to do, is
a matter of commitment and priorities. The person who makes time
for herself has learned that her small action makes a big difference
to her self-esteem and her life. The person who never can find
the time, who is always trying but never accomplishing, has given
up before she began through her lack of commitment. This person
believes her actions make very little difference.

Procrastination is a well-known syndrome to depressed persons.
For women who have been taught to be helpless, dependent, and
fearful, procrastination is a particularly acute problem. We have
been taught to wait, to hesitate, to put other's needs first, to re-
hearse, but not to act. We punish ourselves, pospone our needs, and
convince ourselves that any action in our behalf would be useless.

As we procrastinate, we learn that we cannot trust ourselves.
Each time we make a promise to ourselves that we do not keep, we
reaffirm our own helplessness. We experience not just the helplessness of being unable to control outside influences, but also the helplessness of not being able to control ourselves. Our depression

becomes a grief over the loss of ourselves, and our ability to act in our own behalf.

Procrastination is an outward manifestation of learned helplessness. Some may call it paralysis while others may call it laziness, but it might be more helpful to think of it as passivity, helplessness, or simply "not doing." It is as if we are forever waiting for our lives to begin, waiting for someone or something to force us into doing that which for some reason we feel we cannot do.

Basically, we fear doing for ourselves, forcing ourselves to take those first steps because to initiate implies a belief in ourselves and the ability to change our lives for the better. To force change in ourselves, we must give up the illusions that our actions don't matter. To stop procrastinating, we must admit we have the capacity to and deserve to succeed. Instead we wait—for the willpower to arrive, for the creative inspiration, or for a sign from above. We distract ourselves with others and then blame them for our procrastination. We drink too much, work too much, sleep too little or too much; then we try to stop drinking, working, and sleeping rather than begin whatever we are avoiding and desperately need to do.

Often depressed women complain of having no energy. They tell me this as they chew their nails, fidget, and spend hours worrying over someone else's problems. There is tremendous avoidance here, but there is also energy. Women have the energy—undirected energy —so, to begin dealing with procrastination, we must start by finding out what we are afraid of. What will happen if we lose the weight, write the book, begin to look for a new job, or tell our husbands off?

We must also understand our addiction to waiting and our need of being forever helpless. Then we can deal with the more positive aspects of developing good habits and controlling our time.

Procrastination and Others

We, as women, have been taught for so long to put other's needs first that any new plan we develop to solve our problems is easily laid aside when someone else is in need. After dealing with mother's crisis on the phone, daughter's need for a freshly ironed blouse, a confrontation with the repairman who keeps claiming to have fixed the washer which is *still* not working, it is not too hard to lose sight of newly set goals, much less the plan to get there. In between crises-collecting, we often find ourselves saying, "Now, where *was* I?" only to remember and then berate ourselves for procrastinating.

It is easy to fill our lives and our time with other people's problems. Before we can make some significant changes or even know what we want, we must take control of our time and our energy. Without this, we are like a piece of clay, forever being shaped and reshaped in response to the needs of others, without time for the artist in us to pick up the tools and sculpt our own lives. Without control of our time, we are nothing more than responsive beings, never taking action ourselves; reacting only to our environment while reinforcing our deep-seated sense of helplessness.

Our first commitment must be to take time to ourselves, to determine who we are, what we want, where we are going, and even what we are feeling. We must first be assertive enough to take time for ourselves. We need time to plan, daydream, relax, research, talk to friends, experiment, and listen to ourselves. If we shortchange ourselves here, nothing else can work for us. If we are generous here, fiercely disciplined in our need and our right to take time for ourselves, then there will be few, if any, self-imposed limits on who we can be. If we cannot and will not face this issue, then we are not willing or ready to face ourselves and take responsibility for our lives. In our inaction, we have made a very clear statement that we would rather be miserable and complain (or play the stoic martyr), rather than change and be happy.

Don't try to find the time; *make* the time. This is the tenet of controlling your time. Make time early in the morning before anyone is awake, or late at night when others are asleep. Plan what you are going to think about before you make that hour's worth of driving or spend forty-five minutes in a waiting room at the dentist's office. Use a tape recorder when you can't write—while driving, in the bathtub, or doing dishes. (Tape recorders are a great way to handle correspondence—especially to long-distance relatives). Otherwise, write things down, but don't overwhelm yourself with an endless list of "shoulds." Prioritize, take it in small steps, and be sure to reward yourself for your progress.

What? You can't? Then, let's face it, it's not that you can't, but that you won't. There is a part of you that desperately wants to hide and stay hidden, a part of you that has also invested in not changing, not knowing what you really want, feel, or think. Maybe your husband wouldn't approve; maybe you're afraid of failing.

I can't guess from here, but I do strongly suggest that if you cannot seem to take this first step, this commitment, or if the idea alone terrifies you, then you should find a good counselor. Can you commit that much time—an hour a week to yourself?

Procrastination and Waiting

Women are particularly prone to procrastinate because so much of any woman's life is spent waiting. Though roles and mores have changed significantly in the past few years, women and girls are still waiting. As we wait, we learn to accept helplessness through pain, frustration, and unresolvable problems.

We wait for Mom to do it for us. We wait for our breasts to grow. We wait for boys to get old enough. We wait for our periods to start. We wait to be asked to the prom. We wait to be accepted by a college. We wait for the prospective employer to call. We wait for a new lover to call. We wait for a lover to have more time for us. We wait to be asked to marry. We wait for a raise or a promotion. We wait for a baby to be born. We wait for our husbands to come home. We wait for our husbands to repair the washer. We wait for the children to go to school. We wait for the children to grow and leave home. We wait for our periods to end, for the hot flashes to be over. We wait for some kind of recognition. We wait for our husbands to retire. We wait to die.

We are sleeping beauties waiting frozen in a trance for the kiss of the prince that will magically begin our lives and transform reality into the fairy tale we were weaned on. We were often pro-tected from the real world and sold a bill of goods, a sugarplum-fairy-soft-safe world that has no relationship to the world today as it truly is.

Ill-equipped to deal with the problems we must face today, when frightened or stressed we regress to a childlike state, feeling overwhelmed and paralyzed with fear, wishing and hoping that we will wake up from this bad dream.

So we procrastinate, and we wait. Life will begin tomorrow, we tell ourselves. We know what we need to do, but we ignore reality as we were so effectively trained to do. The longer we wait, the more helpless we become, the more we realize there is no one to rescue us, and the more we attempt to find someone or manipulate someone into doing just that. When this too fails, rather than motivating us into acting in our own behalf, we passively go into mourning.

It is not uncommon to spend more energy trying to find a replacement decision-maker in our lives than attempting to solve our own problems. For many women, finding a replacement is all too easy. As others more willingly rescue us from our problems, both helplessness and our procrastination habit are reinforced. We again learn that if we wait long enough, someone will take care of our problems for us.

Of course, other people's decisions about our lives are not our decisions, and often these decisions are hard for us to live with. But the instant relief of overwhelming anxiety provided by someone rescuing us is more rewarding than any far-off feeling that we might have done better for ourselves if we had made our own decisions. The next time a decision needs to be made or a change initiated, we will stall, procrastinate, complain, and wait for someone else to rescue us again.

Procrastination and Fear

Fear feeds on procrastination as much as our habitual helplessness and need to wait. We are taught not to take risks, to distrust our decision-making ability, and to be extremely cautious of upsetting the status quo.

As women facing decisions, we are full of "what ifs." No matter how simple the decision or action appears, nightmarish outcries plague us. Remember "I Love Lucy" on TV? No matter how small the decision, it always created a disaster. Like this fictional role model from TV, we learned to fear everything that would require new behaviors from us. A washer needs changing, and we imagine a kitchen full of water two feet deep. A nut needs tightening on a bike, and suddenly the bike is falling apart. We fear and remember every comical detail as if it were real.

Then there are all the horror stories. We learn from mother, the news, and the multitude of police/detective television shows that revolve around the theme of some adventurous woman who has just been murdered, raped, or mutilated. Each story reinforces our fear of the Boogie Man and further perpetuates the cycle of fear and procrastination.

The media have a tremendous impact on our lives. We sincerely begin to believe that taking any risk or independent action will bring dire consequences. Beyond anticipating these kind of fictitious consequences, there are other consequences to our taking independent actions. Some are more reality-based than others, such as fear of losing a spouse or a lover's approval if we become more independent.

Finally, we must face the very real fear that many of those closest to us will find our helplessness attractive. If we become more decisive, more assertive and self-directed, this action will pose a threat to those relationships. Our lack of ability to take action and our dependency on others feeds their sense of self-worth while slowly depleting our strength. So we procrastinate, rather than face the disapproval or upset the status quo of the relationship itself. Sooner or later though, with this particular fear of ending procrastination, we must choose between their security or our self-esteem.

On Self-Discipline

There is this word called discipline. It is most unfortunate that, in English, discipline and punishment are used interchangeably. William Glasser calls it "positive addiction"—not much of an improvement semantically. Whether we call it willpower, force, or discipline, at some point we must get strict with ourselves. We can make the task more appealing, such as fixing gourmet diet foods. We can reward ourselves for each hour of writing with an hour of play.

But somewhere we will have to force ourselves against our childlike resistance.

No one said that it would be easy. Procrastination is not a simple habit to change. It is all too easy to slip into blaming our procrastination on various distractions, telling ourselves that somehow we will find the time next week. Procrastination can be overcome one day at a time. More than anything, procrastination is an addictive habit that causes almost complete loss of control over our lives.

Some Practical Suggestions to Control Your Addiction to Procrastination

1. Make a list of excuses you use to procrastinate, such as: "I can't because . . ."; "I don't feel like it now because . . ."; "I will do it when . . ."; "Who needs me?"; "I'd rather be . . .". Make it as elaborate and as embarrassingly explicit as possible. Add to it whenever you notice a new excuse and keep it all in a place where you will see it often. Whenever you find yourself hedging, check in and find out where you are using it. Then go ahead and hedge. Don't criticize yourself.

2. Meditate. Visualize yourself doing the activity. Always put it into positive terms. For example, don't see yourself as not eating. Instead, see yourself as eating delicious low-calorie foods, exercising, and having the figure you want. Give yourselves affirmations to say over and over, like "I am getting thinner and more energetic every day."

3. Make whatever behavior you need to change into a program. Make a time-continuum contract with yourself, i.e., commit yourself to writing four hours a day, or eat only 1000 calories a day and exercise every Monday, Wednesday, and Saturday. Make it realistic. Reward yourself continually, daily or hourly, whatever it takes. The rewards don't need to be elaborate; a phone call to a friend can be a reward; so can a bubble bath. Find as many things as possible that appeal to the sensory-oriented child in you. For working mothers and women, time alone is often the best reward. Whenever your mind starts to rebel, take a break and reward yourself, preferably with some form of physical exercise like dancing to music.

Then return to the task. Change settings as often as necessary and change to different aspects of the same task as well. It's important that you don't get bored or feel confined by the task. Learn to make the task attractive. Think of how parents manipulate their children. If Johnny doesn't like to eat his vegetables, it does no good to berate him or force him. The more unpleasantness associated with the vegetables, the more he will not want to eat them. His parents may, however, get somewhere if they bribe Johnny by fixing him an extra-special dessert; or they may make the vegetables more attractive by disguising them as a more appealing dish.

When dealing with your own procrastination, you are essentially dealing with the rebellious child in all of us who is whining, "But I don't want to" along with various excuses. It is important to teach this child that it is more pleasant to be cooperative than to rebel, and that work can be fun. If you tell any child he "should" do this or that, you automatically lose. Instead, tell yourself you want to diet, exercise, write, or paint; even if you don't really believe it. Or say, "I know I don't want to do this, but I'm going to do it anyway so I can have (*reward*.)" Be sure to eliminate the word "work" from your internal language. "Work" automatically brings to mind images of unpleasantness. Tell yourself you're going to play at being a lawyer, exercising, being studious, seeing how fast you can clean the house to rock music, etc.

4. Learn to simplify—be aware that organization makes things easier. Do two things at once as much as possible, i.e., cleaning out that purse while talking on the phone. Constantly question how you expended your energy by asking "why?," "what for?," "How can I make this simple?"

5. Question the things you habitually procrastinate about. Ask yourself why you avoid this task. What does avoiding this task prove to you about yourself? What usually happens when you avoid this task? For example, avoiding bill payment may occur because it's boring, forces you to think about money, or makes you be responsible. Not paying those bills gives a temporary reprieve from these issues and gives the illusion of having more money than you actually do. But if you avoid paying bills, you usually overspend, and sooner or later, suffer some form of punishment; i.e., the phone

company sends a threatening letter or the electricity is turned off. Then you can feel like the helpless victim and berate yourself for constant laziness, reaffirming your image of irresponsibility.

6. Coordinate and plan. Again, the extra energy of planning ahead saves energy, and keeps you directed and motivated. Have lists of "have to's" and "want to's"—plan the night before, once a week, once a month. Checking things off a list gives a feeling of accomplishment and helps fight the procrastination habit.

7. Learning to delegate is an important skill to learn toward effective time management. Trade tasks with friends to save time and energy. For example: I will do your laundry if you do my shopping. Trade services with friends or consider hiring someone to do the tasks you tend to avoid. You'll make it closer to Wonder Woman status by learning to delegate tasks rather than trying to do it all by yourself.

8. Give up perfectionism. Perfectionism is one of the greatest obstacles of accomplishment and feeds procrastination. If nothing less than perfect will do, then everything becomes a near impossible monumental task. Perfectionism consumes incredible amounts of time and creates anxiety and pain, not only in yourself but in those you work with as well.

9. Give up the fantasy that you "work well under pressure." This is the self-deluding motto of a true procrastinator. What this person is really saying is that "I don't work at all unless I'm forced to and cannot procrastinate any longer." Admit your problem with procrastination and that working under looming deadlines causes sloppy work as well as ulcers and frayed nerves.

10. Learn to schedule your time creatively to fit your body's rhythms. Think about how you like to work, under what type of conditions, with how much rest. Experiment with different types of scheduling to avoid burn-out. For instance, have one busy week and one catch-up week at work. Schedule appointments accordingly. Or, try doing all the unpleasant tasks in the morning to get them out of the way.

Be sure to schedule "off" time to rest and be alone. Don't underestimate your needs by not scheduling "alone" time. This is very important to your physical and mental health, your work, and your relationships. Also, begin to schedule exercise periods, even if it's a brisk walk. If you're unsure about your biorhythm, keep a journal for a week or two; make notes about every two hours of waking time regarding your mood and energy level. Rhythms do change, depending upon stress, diet, and other factors. Think of your body and calendar as tools that were meant to work together rather than independently.

11. Develop both short-range and long-range goals. Use your fantasies, dreams, and past experiences to tune in to long-range goals that "fit" you.

12. Avoid overscheduling at all costs. The reasons for overscheduling vary. Sometimes we can't seem to say no, sometimes we can't delegate; oftentimes, we just haven't prioritized our activities. Sometimes overscheduling is a way to escape from chronic depression. We fill our lives too full, so we won't have to think or feel.

Admit you're a workaholic. It's nothing to hide from. Keep your workaholic self in check. Don't let the zealot in you take over your scheduling. Be gentle and generous with your schedule, making sure you have lots of time to rest and play. Mark off half days, full days, weeks, or whatever is necessary to avoid "burn-out." If you are one of those people who keeps going until they burn out and use this as an excuse to cut back, then be aware. Try instead to go for consistency and endurance by scheduling sanely and not taking on too much. Ask yourself constantly, "What am I trying to prove?"

If none of this works, then it's safe to assume that you are a "burn-out addict." You can allow yourself time when your body and nerves are so frayed that you cannot function, a workaholic martyr who's allowed time to herself only when she is nearly dead or crazy. If this is your pattern, seek help from a friend or counselor. Put your scheduling in their hands for a while. Check in with them regularly regarding your next week's schedule to see that it's as sane as possible and to help you establish priorities. Finally, and most importantly, learn to say "no."

13. Identify the person and activities that consistently steal precious minutes and learn to be assertive with them. If "the guilties" grab

you whenever you attempt to say "no," determine what role or myth you are trying to live up to: the "dutiful daughter," "socialite," "workhorse," or "earth mother." Don't buy other people's guilt trips and be aware of how they try to manuipulate you.

Above all, remember that owning your time is the first and most important step to owning yourself and your life.

chapter eleven

Rethinking Relationships

Women have been raised to define themselves in relation to others. We have been taught that to be a successful woman one must love and be loved. A woman without love is considered a failure.

Given this background it is not surprising that the central issues in most women's lives involves problems of loving versus identity, or dependence versus independence. This conflict takes us to the heart of the matter. Peele, in *Love and Addiction,* correlated a variety of studies about the addictive personality type. He found that the central underlying problem common to all "addicts" was an unresolved conflict of dependence versus autonomy. Given the feminine traits found in this personality type (see chapter on Bondage) and the sex-role training of females in this culture, it is a realistic assumption that women are predisposed to be addicted to love. Is it a fantasy of love that keeps women so spellbound? If so, its a spell that can entrap a woman throughout her life, from which she often wakes up bitter, old and alone only to find she has sacrificed her life by chasing an elusive shadow, never really knowing herself. Some wake up earlier than others, some decide upon an either/or choice between autonomy or love, and some never wake up at all.

Let's take a look at how this enchantment began and what we learned about love.

For both females and males, the first experience with love is during infancy, when we are totally dependent on our mothers for our very survival. In infancy we are also very vulnerable both physically and emotionally, because of our dependency, size, and inability to problem-solve. The infant is completely egocentric, totally concerned with its own needs and not the least concerned with the needs of others. The mother is the all-giving, all-sacrificing supplier of the infant's needs. In the early part of their relationship the mother appears to be such a bottomless source of love and comfort that the infant cannot distinguish where she or he ends and the mother begins; that distinction is learned later. During this period we learn a passive, egocentric version of love; a love that involves receiving, having all our needs continually met, and a love that also involves feelings of vulnerability and dependency. Some of us leave this period more secure than others, just as some of us experience the transition from infancy to childhood with more or less trauma than others. What is important here is that if we experienced infancy as a state of emotional or physical deprivation, if we leave infancy feeling insecure and unaccepted, we will often seek to recapture this unmet experience in a loving relationship later in life.

As we move into childhood we experience rules, limitations, and expectations for the first time. Some children experience these expectations as skills to be mastered from which they may gain a feeling of competency. Other children may experience this period as a withdrawal of the unconditional love they received as infants. As individuals move through childhood into adolescence they are faced with another set of decisions regarding loving: either to move forward into a form of loving that involves giving as well as receiving or to move backward by manipulating others into the all-giving or dependent love they experienced in infancy. Many of us know no other form of love other than that which we experienced as children. But the love between adults is not and should not be the same kind of love that exists between mother and infant. Adult love is based primarily on independence, meaning the ability to meet one's own emotional and physical needs. This is not to be confused with the phoney independence many dependent people use as a defense, which involves denial of one's emotional needs (or even physical needs) until "the right one comes along." It is difficult for girls/women to develop the independence necessary for adult love or what Erich Fromm refers to as "mature love" when we are being encouraged to be dependent, childlike, and the love object for others. It is even more difficult for women to become responsible for our emotional needs when we are being lulled to a regressive sleep by the fairy tale of Prince Charming who will do all the growing up and becoming responsible "for" us.

By early pubescence, men and women have begun to see members of the opposite sex as objects of love. There is only the relatively short period of childhood when boys and girls are able to view each other as both friends and persons. By pubescence this perspective gives way to the more narrow viewpoint that labels and ranks each person as desirable, invisible, or disgusting. From here on both sexes will develop peculiarly distorted perspectives of each other as well as an equally distorted form of communicating with one another full of caution and bluffs.

We accept all this as reasonable and normal. We see young children attempting to emulate this game as cute or endearing. What may be cute is the openness and hopefulness of young love. But what is equally sad is how young and quickly we learn to see the opposite sex as objects—a screen—on which we can project a fantasy instead of a real person with real fallibilities. As a culture we believe that love is blind, that love should be blind. Yet if we truly love another for whom they are, we are not blind. Rather, if we honestly learn to love other people, we can see all of their weaknesses and faults. We may choose, because of our love, to accept these weaknesses. But if we do not see another's faults, then we do not know them. And if we do not know them, then we cannot *really* love them.

As we move through adolescence our desire to love and be loved becomes more and more focused on the fantasy of one person who will meet all our needs; friends take more and more of a backseat to the fantasy lover. The friends on whom we were once so dependent, with whom we had once spent so much time and energy, now become mere devices for entertainment whenever there is free time. It is only when the belief in the fantasy lover is properly laid to rest that we will reexamine the meaning of friendship in our lives.

Just as we lose touch with our friends, we also begin to lose touch with ourselves and our needs. This search for "the one and only" often becomes tedious, fraught with panic and feelings of rejection.

Motivated by weariness and fear we often feel the need to hurry and find someone to settle this uncomfortable part of our life. In more active pursuit, we find someone and out of the sheer relief of acceptance, we gratefully fall in love. The movie begins, and lo and behold, our "someone" miraculously becomes all that we have ever wanted, the "fantasy lover." Or so we believe, until our own needs (and sense of reality) rises up and turns off the movie projector. We are then faced with, to our dismay, not a god or goddess, not the perfect parent, but a real human being, vulnerable, feeling equally betrayed and guilt-ridden for not being able to live up to an impossible standard. At this point the relationship usually dissolves or deteriorates into a cold war of resentment. Just as we experience the sensation of falling in love as uncontrolled euphoria, we experience the sensation of falling out of love, or rejection, as an uncontrolled feeling of lack of self-worth, agitation, and depression. Likening these processes to the experiences of taking a strong drug and clinical withdrawal is perhaps more than a metaphor. It may well be that the body/mind actually experiences these processes as the same; identical in the relief each provides, the addictive nature of both, and the extreme sense of deprivation when the dependency is not met.

Not all loving relationships are so self-destructive. Love can be an enhancing education or a neurotic "fix"; the choice is ours. This choice depends on whether we choose to love out of the abundance of self-love and independence, or as a neurotic, substitute, self-love so that we may remain dependent.

Relationships enhance in a healthy way only if they are *positive* relationships. A positive relationship is one in which contact with that person makes us feel better about ourselves. Not just safer, less lonely, or needed, but actually better about ourselves and our potential. All too often we are so busy meeting the needs of others and basking in the false glory of being needed that we never stop to think whether a relationship is meeting our needs or simply depleting us.

We often rationalize staying in a relationship that is not positive by telling ourselves it is "not that bad." Whether the relationship in question is that of a friendship or of an intimate nature, to invest time and energy into a relationship that gives us little in return is a destructive act toward our self-esteem. To stay in a "not bad" relationship implies the best we deserve is a "not good" relationship. It is as if we are saying to ourselves that it is good enough that we are not being badly abused and that we have no right to respond to our own needs. There is also a simple law of time economics operating here. We have only so much time in our day-to-day lives to devote to forming and maintaining relationships. If we use that time to continue relationships that are less than good, relationships where our needs are not being met, then it is very unlikely we will ever find better relationships that more adequately meet our needs. In holding on to "not bad" relationships, we are sentencing ourselves to a lifetime of unmet needs and emotional–social deprivation.

We must reach our maturity by replacing infantile or childlike dependencies with self-love and independent action. Many of us have not allowed ourselves adolescence, that process of letting go, resolving childhood conflict, and learning to love and trust in ourselves, *independent* of the behavior of others.

If we are to let go of the fantasy lover (and parent) and move into a more realistic and adult love, we must rid ourselves of the need for approval from others as a method to prove our self-worth. Self-worth is not real or stable if it must be proven. Self-worth, or self-love, simply is. We do not love children only when they are good enough and desert them when they are bad. We love our children good or bad, independent of their behavior. But we are often not so generous with ourselves. Self-love tends to be conditional; we are supportive of ourselves only when we are performing up to some bizarre standard we have set for ourselves. We must learn to nurture ourselves in the way a loving, warm, good parent nurtures a child.

We must learn to become the fantasy parent, the perfect parent we always wanted, to ourselves. We must be able to care for ourselves not just in the rudimentary ways, giving ourselves only emotionally spartan lives. Rather, we must be generous to and sometimes forceful with ourselves. Only in this way can we move away from seeking parental substitutes (or love objects) in loving relationships and learn to love another freely, independently, completely, without self-sacrifice or the need to control.

Conscious Love

Most people, especially women, are extremely resistant to the idea of using their conscious minds to make decisions about loving relationships. We have been raised with the myth that loving must somehow be an emotional, unconscious, and mystical experience. We relate "falling in love" with being out of control, unable to think straight or barely function. Given this image, which likens love to near madness, it is not surprising that we resist the idea that to love in a healthy way we must learn to use both our rational minds and our emotions.

Many of us have experienced the process of the rational mind coming alive in the painful decision-making process when a relationship is bad. But few of us use our rational minds to help us define what our values are or what kind of relationships we *do* want.

Women try to be incredibly malleable, attempting to transform and mold themselves at will to become the perfect mate for any man they might desire. We have learned since early childhood how to be what others want. In fact, so much of a woman's life is spent acting and giving unconscious performances, that it is all too easy for any woman to wake up one day wondering who she is. Because of this malleability and motivated by the desire to please, women often end up compromising their values in relationships that don't really work for them. This tendency breeds resentment, hostility, and depression.

An act of self-love, as well as the concern for those we love, is to clarify our values. If we compromise ourselves in loving relationships, we will never forgive our partners or ourselves and this resentment will contaminate the love. Each of us has values regarding loving relationships. Each of us has a fantasy or ideal and each of us has a bottom-line. If we sell ourselves short, below our "bottom-line," we will experience discomfort and self-depreciation. Self-sacrifice is not the way to achieve love; it is the way to destroy love. Nor is self-sacrifice attractive. A groveling pup elicits no affection, only pity at best, and often it seems to invite a kick. Self-sacrificing, self-effacing love elicits the same response, as noted in this quote by George Bernard Shaw:

> Although romantic idealists generally insist on self-surrender as an indispensable element in true womanly love, its repulsive effect is well known and feared in practice by both sexes. The extreme instance is the reckless self-abandonment as seen in infatuation of passionate sexual desire. Everyone who becomes the object of that infatuation shrinks from it instinctively. Love loses its charm when it is not free, and whether the compulsion is that of custom, law or of infatuation, the effect is the same: it becomes valueless. The desire to give inspires no affection unless there is also the power to withhold; and the successful wooer, in both sexes alike, is the one who can stand out for honorable conditions and failing that, go without! [1]

The last lines of this quote imply self-confidence and self-love. One of the largest obstacles women must overcome, in order to achieve mental health, independence, equality and self-confidence, is the belief that our sense of worth is based on a loving relationship. As long as this holds true we will compromise ourselves (if not destroy ourselves) in the name of love and choose those we love not from a rational perspective of complimentary values but rather out of quiet desperation. No relationship can work when one person has so much to lose. For we have truly lost this game before it is begun if we are looking for in others what we must give ourselves. Love is a cop-out, a dependency, a destructive game, as long as we allow ourselves to focus on the love object at the expense of ourselves. Loving can also be a lesson in growth, a spiritual path that is the extension of the abundance of self-love and strength. Erich Fromm tells us in *The Art of Loving:*

> Love is not primarily a relationship to a specific person. It is an attitude, an orientation of character which determines the related-

ness of a person—not toward one "object" of love. If a person loves only one other person and is indifferent to his fellow man, his love is not love but selfish attachment, or an enlarged egotism. Yet most people believe that love is constituted by the object, not by the faculty. In fact, they even say that it is proof of the intensity of their love when they do not love anybody but the "loved" person. If I truly love one person I love all persons, I love the world, I love life. If I can say to somebody else, "I love you" I must be able to say "I love you everybody, I love through you the world, I love you, also myself." [2]

Through self-knowledge and courage loving can be a daily lesson that begins with ourselves and moves outward into the world. This is the merging between the love of the self and the love of another, and spiritual love or the love of the world. Feelings of greed and deprivation are with us only when we love another and exclude ourselves and the world. When we focus on the experience of loving, rather than a specific person, love is fulfilling and enhancing.

Some practical suggestions on rethinking relationships and increasing self-love:

1. Make a list of the rules you impose on relationships, i.e., "My lover should know what I need without having to be told" or "All loving relationships should be monogamous" or "It's acceptable to have friends only of the same sex as me." See how many rules you can come up with, looking at all areas of loving relationships including sexuality, time spent together and apart, communication, feelings, etc. After you have the most complete list you can create, go over the rules and ask yourself whether or not you want to believe in each rule and whether or not it is benefiting you to believe in each rule. Make some conscious choices about your rules regarding loving relationships.

2. Mature love is not fixated toward one person; it is an attitude and a state of being toward yourself and the whole world. Many spiritual leaders refer to loving as "having an open heart" versus "having a closed heart." Many body therapists refer to being closed or hard versus being open or soft. Spend some time experiencing the sensation of loving. Imagine how your body feels when you're in love. Allow yourself to open, soften, and feel safe. Learn through your body that love is an attitude, a sensation, not an act or a feeling elicited by one person.

3. Be aware that there is no difference between parental love, sexual love, the love of friends, and spiritual love. Stop categorizing love—

allow yourself to experience love in each of these areas of your life. There are not different types of love, only different rules that we impose on love.

4. Give up the fantasy that there is one person who can meet all your needs, and then sacrificing those needs when they are not met. Instead, through good, close friendships, creatively learn to meet all of your needs.

5. Discuss with a friend or do some writing about your early dating experiences. Include any messages you received from your parents.

6. Many of us maintain an unconscious belief that we can be lovable or capable but not both. If this is a problem for you, reprogram yourself by using the affirmation, "I am a lovable and capable person" or "I am becoming more lovable and capable every day."

7. Most of us spend our lives either being "hooked" on commitment or avoiding being "hooked" through lack of commitment. Avoidance is not the answer. The answer lies in yourself, in realizing there is nothing anyone can give you that you are not capable of giving yourself. As long as you maintain the belief that someone else can, will, and should make you happy, you will continue to have desolate and confused relationships at the expense of your self-esteem.

8. The fear of facing old age alone is common. As an exercise, design an old-age plan for yourself that does not include a spouse.

9. Keep an ongoing list of fun things to do with a friend and on your own.

10. During periods of conflict in a relationship, ask yourself, "What aspect of my childhood do these feelings remind me of?"

11. Be aware of the qualities you want but just can't seem to find in a lover. Ask yourself if you had such a lover what attitudes would you have to change about yourself.

12. Here's a series of fill-in-the-blanks that you might find helpful: "I need more of _____. I could get more of _____ by _____. My lover needs more of _____. I could help him (or her) with this by _____."

13. Sometimes we punish ourselves by chosing a lover who doesn't meet our needs. Be aware of how you use your relationships with others to hurt yourself.

14. It is very common for a couple to punish each other subtly for various wrongdoings rather than face conflict. Work to deal with conflict openly rather than by punishing or withholding.

15. Ask yourself, "What do I find most attractive and most negative

about my lover? How are these attributes part of myself or how have I repressed these aspects of myself?"

16. Make a series of statements that are complaints regarding your relationship, then change the statements to own them as your problem. (For example, change "He is insensitive" to "I am insensitive.") See if the shoe fits.

17. Often our self-image is such that we don't believe we deserve a satisfying loving relationship. Start reprogramming yourself by using the affirmation, "I deserve to be loved."

18. Give your lover and friends a clear idea of what you need when you are upset. This information will help everyone involved.

19. Learn to put the time and energy into your friendships so that these relationships will be truly satisfying and growth-enhancing.

20. Awareness and action are what keep a relationship out of a rut.

21. Sometimes it is necessary to choose consciously to stay out of love for a specific period of time. This gives you time to focus on yourself and to be weaned from the addictive aspects of love.

22. When you sense a relationship is moving too fast, consciously choose to slow things down.

23. Purposely embark on a campaign to delete victim behavior from your life.

24. Learn to negotiate versus sacrificing yourself and feeling resentful about it later.

25. Do alone the things you normally do with someone else. Become your own best friend and lover.

26. Finally, remember that you must teach others to value you and what you need. This can be done only when you truly value yourself as a unique individual and face who you are, clarifying between needs and wants, defining what you want in a relationship and developing a repertoire of skills to meet those needs creatively.

chapter twelve

Money

Money is a symbol via which we exchange energy, time, and merchandise. Economics is the game we play, and money is the means by which we keep score of how well we are doing. But this is not a children's game. It is a game with serious results and repercussions. Part of this game is known as the politics of money. In this country the politics of money translates to "those who have the most money acquire the largest voice and get to change the rules we are all forced to play by." This phenomenon is not likely to change. Money does carry with it a certain amount of power, to dominate or help others, to influence or to brainwash. Much of this depends on your point of view, some of this depends on your morals.

Given this structure, it is easy to see how those who have the least money often are heard the least. There is no doubt that women, children, minorities, and the elderly are frequently hurt by this system, but the hurt is usually unintentional neglect rather than some form of direct abuse.

This is an important concept. It is all too easy for us to see our present financial situation as something someone (or a group of people) is doing to us. When we feel this way, it follows that we begin to feel that those who are "doing it to us" *owe* us. This cultivates both hatred and passivity. We hate because "they" are not giving "us" the debt "they" owe. It cultivates passivity because we tend to wait to be given or somehow reserve fully taking on the responsibility of changing our financial situation. We halfheartedly look for work, expecting the worst, and find ourselves unable to visualize a better life. The hatred and bitterness permeates us. We bitterly believe a better life is for "them," not "us," and so we give up. We look at those who "have" with envy, resentment, and suspicion, while we secretly vow that we will never be like "them." I am not defending starvation, unequal education, or neglect of the elderly and minorities. But I am suggesting that our attitudes have a great deal to do with whether or not we will remain in our present financial situation or whether we will change it. If we want to change things, we cannot waste time bemoaning "Oh poor me, look what they're doing to me." We cannot *afford* to cultivate hate, resentment, and helplessness. If we want to change things, we must begin with ourselves, working consistently to improve our financial situations so that we as a group (women/minorities) will be heard and have the power to create political and economic change.

Women and Money

Traditional myth tells us that women do not need to support themselves because men will do it for them. This is of course far from the present-day realities. Women can no longer expect to be "taken care of" on a lifelong basis. Many women have come to the realization that "being taken care of" costs a heavy price in loss of self-esteem, inequitable relationships, and the ultimate financial insecurity of dependency. Despite the realities of divorce, single motherhood, death or illness of a spouse, and the need for dual incomes due to inflation, many women cling to the idea that they shouldn't have to be concerned about supporting themselves. Many women spend their entire lives expecting someone else to "help" them financially, while remaining poor and unskilled, waiting for a prince charming or a fairy godmother to bestow wealth upon them. They learn how to get by and tell themselves that getting by is good enough. Or they learn how to spend, and tell themselves that finding bargains or shopping is good enough. They may work at a job they dislike or find boring and tell themselves that "a job is a job." Very rarely do women think about money in terms of a goal that they have the power to reach. Most women don't want to think about money or believe that they could have more if they were willing to change their attitudes about money. This chapter challenges the negative attitudes and beliefs about money that may be interfering with your ability to make more money.

The following myths about money are a distillation of the myths presented by Phil Laut in *Money Is My Friend* and my own ideas.

Some Common Myths About Money

1. *Money is evil.* This myth contends that money is the root of all that is evil. Money is seen as inherently bad, therefore, it should be avoided.

2. *There is only so much money to go around, so if you are rich you are causing someone else's poverty.* This is an interesting fantasy, as the government prints more money all the time.

3. *It is more righteous to be poor.* It is somehow considered a sign of saintliness to be poor because it means you are not guilty of causing someone else's poverty. This also comes from the belief that if your life is a struggle, you will automatically earn your place in heaven.

4. *Education will cause wealth.* This myth contends that a good education will ensure financial success. Millions of educated unemployed people would beg to disagree.

5. *You must work very hard at a boring, awful job in order to make a lot of money.* It is this myth that makes us feel it is impossible to make good money by doing something we enjoy.

6. *If we make a lot of money, we will become greedy, selfish, and money-oriented.* This myth assumes money-making is a negative addiction that we have no ability to control. This belief could be compared to the idea that if we frequently engage in sex, then we will become nymphomaniacs.

7. *It is unfeminine for a woman to be interested in making money.* Here we face the masculine taboo that claims money-making is only for men. The assumption tacked on this myth reads, "Women are therefore relegated either to seeking a man to be the source of their income or to poverty."

Belief in any or all of these myths will block one's ability to achieve financial success, however the individual chooses to define it.

Poverty Games

There are many psychological games we play with ourselves (and others) to justify remaining poor or unstable economically. Each game not only justifies our past and present economic situations, it also explains why we cannot do anything to change our finances in the future. All of these games are forms of self-victimization which claims that we are being controlled by money (or the lack thereof). The first game is called "Poor and Proud." People involved in this game see themselves as martyrs to their poverty or pursuit of financial security. They often let others know how proud they are by playing out some version of "look how hard I try" or "poor me." It is not uncommon for those involved in this game to see themselves as bravely working themselves to the bone for others. This game also becomes an excuse for getting out of a variety of interpersonal responsibilities (such as being responsive to the emotional needs of spouse, children, or friends).

Another game we play with ourselves regarding money is called "Just Getting By." Persons involved in this game are so involved in making ends meet that they have little or no energy left for anything else, especially finding a way to improve their financial situations. This game can be played at any level of income. A high-income person gets involved by overspending via cash or credit. Persons involved in this game don't really believe that they deserve to have enough money. They often rationalize their position by reminding themselves that just getting by is good enough.

The next game that those involved in "poverty consciousness" often play is called "If It Weren't For. . . ." In this game people blame their financial situation on something or someone else. There is always some sort of burden involved that is perceived to be the source of the financial problems. The "burden" may be the loss of a spouse, or a job, poor health, a wrong decision based on bad advice, a child that refuses to grow up, or the economy in general. Whether the burdens are real or imagined, circumstantial or self-perpetuated is unimportant. What is important is that the persons involved in this game use the burdens as excuses to refuse to act in their own behalf so that they can blame their poverty on someone or something else.

"Self-Punishment" is another psychological game we play to justify staying poor. Many of us don't believe we deserve financial comfort or prosperity. Sometimes our feelings of not-deserving have to do with a general feeling of poor self-esteem. But oftentimes these feelings are related to some real or imagined wrongdoing for which we feel we deserve to be punished. The "crime" may refer to a specific childhood event or it may be more nebulous. For instance, children with aloof and disapproving parents often feel as if they are generally bad and children of parents with very high or rigid expectations often feel as if they are bad because they cannot be perfect.

"Almost" is another poverty-conscious game. "Almost" involves working very hard at achieving only to fail at the crucial moment when everything looks rosy. "Almost" is a success-failure cycle that tantalizes the participants into replaying over and over without perceiving the similarity of the pattern. "Almost" informs everyone (including the participants) of the potential and worthiness of the game players, yet when success is within reach they always unconsciously sabotage themselves into last-minute failure.

Sometimes we use poverty to hold onto parents, dependency, and childhood. This game is called "Back to the Womb." These people haven't reconciled themselves to the financial responsibilities (and often the emotional responsibilities) of adulthood. Basically they hope that if they stay poor long enough someone (Mommy, Daddy, Prince or Princess Charming) will come to the rescue so that they can return to the womb-like protection of being taken care of. To give up their poverty would mean that a potential rescuer might not notice how badly they want to and need to be rescued. All too often parents participate in this game by "helping" their children into emotional regression and financial dependency, all the while playing their own version of "If It Weren't for . . . (my adult child who is still financially dependent)."

Another game that relates to the unfinished psychological issues of childhood is what Phil Laut calls "Failing to Get Even" [1] in his book *Money Is My Friend.* "Failing to get Even" is when we fail in terms of work and finances as a method of punishing our parents for some real or imagined wrongdoing. By failing we can rob our parents of the satisfaction of being proud of us and thereby covertly express our anger toward them. This game can also be played with a spouse or society in general. I have seen an example of this in a client who as an adolescent had her heart set on being a doctor. She was told by "someone" that she couldn't be a doctor because she was female. Since that time she has failed in some way at all her career attempts, though she is well-educated and very talented. In this way she is punishing society for its sexism, unfortunately at the expense of herself.

A psychological game we play that keeps us from prosperity has been widely discussed in the last several years. Matina Horner in her studies concluded that many women fear success. Since then other theorists have concluded from their own studies that fear of success is not solely a woman's problem. Whichever the case, it appears that many people fear success. This is often because to succeed means to risk failure. Many people would rather limp along and not try their best rather than face trying their damndest and losing. Others are frightened of the increased expectations people will have of them (and they will have of themselves) if they succeed. Another common fear is that if we succeed we will somehow lose ourselves to our success. This is a fairly realistic fear, because if we succeed we *will* lose, at least in part, our poor self-image and the psychological security of believing we are a failure.

The last game presented here is "Us and Them." I have mentioned this game in the introduction of this chapter. It is when people identify themselves as poor and see the rich as persecuting them. This game can also be reversed, where wealthy people see poor people as the source of all their financial problems (including high taxes). Whichever class is playing the game, they tend to see the other class ("them") as bad, greedy, and lazy. This set of class prejudices makes it impossible for people to: (1) stop blaming and take complete responsibility for themselves financially, (2) let go of their poverty-consciousness and develop the ability to think and act in such a manner as to increase their prosperity, (3) develop the commonality of concern and cooperation necessary to change the political/economic situation.

All classes use this game to justify stealing, welfare and insurance fraud, embezzlement, selfishness, lack of compassion and charity, and poor work performance. As long as we continue to blame and punish we will not be able to work together to find a way to heal ourselves and our country economically.

Survival and Security

We often connect money with our feelings about survival and security. These feelings often go back to our childhood and our early experiences with love. This is why when we are fighting about or worrying about money we are really fighting about or worrying about love and security.

When I have asked clients and students what security means to them the most frequent reply I receive is that security is knowing you can survive the rough times. If this is real security, and I believe it is, then why is it that we delude ourselves into thinking that if we had enough money we would be secure? Insecure people who have not really overcome rough times on their own, fail to learn that security is self-generated. When we have not learned to depend on ourselves, we depend on others to meet our needs. But precisely because this is a dependency, because our security is in someone else's hands, the feeling of security is never met. We remain insatiable, never able to get enough (money, love, reassurance, etc.) because the lesson of self-reliance has not been learned.

It is interesting and helpful to remind ourselves that human beings actually need very little to survive. During a period of several years of desperate poverty I was amazed as to how little food I actually needed and how many things I had once considered necessities (my own place to live, a car, electricity, and a phone) were actually luxuries. I became lean and strong during those years. Somewhere along the way I lost my fears of money and survival, and gained the confidence of knowing I am the creator of my own security.

From Poverty Consciousness to Prosperity Consciousness

Phil Laut suggests that the law of money is that "All human wealth is created in the human mind." [2] I would go a step further and suggest that "all human wealth is created in the human mind and by human action." This is a hard concept to accept. It means giving up on all the blaming and excuses. It means changing our minds about money and changing our beliefs about our capacity to earn money. Finally, it means choosing to make a commitment to earn more and have more money.

What do you have to do to have more money? Well, you won't have to work long hours at something you hate or rob a bank. What you will have to do is consciously work at changing your attitudes (which is the hardest part), develop goals and work consistently toward those goals. Goals and work—sounds hard—but it isn't if you set goals that involve doing activities you enjoy. Yes, you can make money doing something you enjoy. In fact, if you do something you don't enjoy for work, it is almost guaranteed you won't get rich from it. There, I said it, that word that arouses more ruckus than sex, "rich."

Do you deserve to be rich? Do you want to be rich? If you can work through your negative programming enough to answer these questions "yes," then you are well on your way. For those who answer "no" or a very hesitant maybe, remember that first of all, rich can mean anything you wish. How others might choose to interpret the word "rich" might be different from your definition.

Second, if nice people like you don't deserve to be rich, then who does? I bet there are all kinds of positive ways you could use your wealth to help others. If you really care about your fellow human beings and the plight of the poor, then you owe it to yourself and others to earn your wealth so that you can help others out.

Thoughts and Behaviors
that Hold Us Back from Prosperity

Before we go on, here is a list of thoughts and behaviors that disrupt our ability to work toward prosperity. Note which ones apply to you.

1. Clinging to negative thoughts about security and survival.
2. Approval seeking.
3. Lack of self-control or self-discipline.
4. Inability to set limits.
5. Lack of commitment.
6. Inability to be comfortable alone.
7. Inability to relax and have fun.
8. Unfinished psychological problems regarding parents (i.e., "failing to get even").
9. Fear of disapproval.
10. Fear of taking risks.
11. Inability to accept reality or change.
12. Helplessness and apathy.
13. Clinging to childhood.
14. Self-deprivation as a form of self-punishment.
15. Fear of competing with or being better than others (including parents).
16. Fear of loss of control.
17. Negative attitudes about rich people.
18. Fear of failure and/or success.
19. Being compulsively concerned with the problems of others.
20. Improper health habits, i.e., poor nutrition, excessive use of alcohol and drugs, lack of rest.

21. Poor self-image.
22. Lack of assertiveness.
23. Inability to set reasonable goals.
24. Inability to reward oneself.
25. Dependency on others for financial security.

SOME PRACTICAL SUGGESTIONS
FOR BECOMING PROSPEROUS

Now, here are a series of hints, exercises, and important points to help you become prosperous.

1. Remember that money is a symbol that flows into and out of your life.
2. Cultivate your materialistic desires. Materialism, enjoying the things that money can buy, is a positive attribute as long as it truly reflects your values and is balanced with other values, i.e., humanitarianism, spirituality, concern for loved ones, etc. When you admire something, tell yourself, "I can have that!" Imagine the things, experiences, and gifts you would love to buy if you were rich. Be sure to remind yourself that you deserve it.
3. Whenever possible, go first-class to the best restaurant, the best seats in the house, etc. If that means you can't eat junk food out for a month, so be it. It is a better investment of your money to go without and enjoy first-class occasionally, than to go cheap all the time.
4. Give to a local charity regularly no matter how little you can afford.
5. Cleanse your mind and life of negativity and clutter. Clean out your drawers, clean up messy relationships, get rid of nagging tasks that you've been procrastinating about.
6. Learn to brainstorm solutions and think creatively about making money. Let loose of the idea that there is only one way to make money.
7. Learn to be flexible regarding money and work. Those who will ride through economic hard times in style will be those who can be flexible.
8. Get a sense of your parents' financial script. How did they view money and work? Consciously decide if you wish to continue to accept their values.
9. Try these interesting power exercises: (a) Write a letter to money, expressing all your thoughts and feelings; (b) Write a letter to

your parents expressing whatever negative feelings you have toward them regarding your childhood; (c) Write a letter to love expressing all your thoughts and feelings; (d) Write a letter to your sexuality expressing all your thoughts and feelings; (e) Compare the letters circling common themes (you might ask a close friend to review them and do the same).

10. Make a list of those individuals and/or institutions on which you are financially dependent. Remember it is wise to depend only on dependable institutions or people.

11. Learn to sell ideas and yourself. Marketing and sales are the most important economic skills you can acquire next to basic mathematics. To sell an idea, product, or your services: (a) identify the positive points, (b) make the negative points into assets (i.e., your age may make you more reliable), (c) identify your audience (who is likely to buy your product or service?), and (d) "package" your service or product in such a way as to solve a problem of your audience.

12. Learn to use your time effectively and creatively.

13. Think BIG—it is just as easy to make $1,000 as it is $100.

14. Change your image to look more prosperous.

15. Learn to enjoy small pleasures.

16. Pretend you are a millionaire in disguise.

17. Trust that your capacity to earn is limitless.

18. Realize that feeling guilty about spending money indicates a lack of faith in your capacity to create more.

19. Keep a journal for a month of *all* your expenditures to find out where every dime goes.

20. Give up your belief in failure. There is no failure, only success and not succeeding *yet*.

21. Make a list of five things you could do in your job to improve it.

22. This is an adaptation of suggestions of working at what you love. Even if you have a job you love, try this exercise just to keep yourself economically limber:

    (a) Write a list of your ten favorite activities.

    (b) Review and come up with at least three ways you could possibly make money doing each.

    (c) Pick a favorite and polish the idea.

    (d) Make a list of ten things you are willing to do in order to make your idea work.

    (e) Break this list down further while adding a time contingency to each.

    (f) Make a commitment to stick with your plan until you've made $100.

23. Finally, and most importantly, use affirmations to change your poverty-consciousness to prosperity-consciousness. Try such affirmations as: I deserve to be rich. I am growing more prosperous every day. There is no limit to my prosperity. I am becoming more prosperous, peaceful, and creative every day. (More affirmations can be found in Phil Laut's book *Money Is My Friend* and Jerry Gillies' book, *Moneylove*.) Don't underestimate the power of affirmations. Affirmations work like magic to powerfully influence the mind and the ability to create prosperity. So repeat after me, "I deserve to be rich!"

chapter thirteen

Upkeep of the Body

Traditionally, Western culture has seen the mind and body as separate. It is only recently that we have begun seriously to conceive of the mind and body as a whole unit. Yet as a culture we still disown our bodies in many ways. We take care of our bodies poorly, especially in times of stress, and we feel betrayed and angry when our bodies are not healthy or less than perfect. Our bodies are our tools and homes. Our bodies are the outward manifestations of ourselves which respond well to good treatment and which will eventually wear out and die. We can take care of ourselves, ignore ourselves, or even make war on ourselves; the choice is ours.

Women in particular, due to years of comparing, competing, and feeling grossly inadequate, often disown their bodies and are painfully aware of each flaw. We often use fat and illness to hide from ourselves our sexuality and ourselves. We starve and gorge ourselves. We complain about our flaws and exhibit our assets, but rarely do we truly accept our bodies or ourselves.

To own our bodies, to calm ourselves, to unlearn destructive habits and relearn healthful ones are acts of self-love, acceptance, responsibility, and growth. When we change our attitude about our bodies and take responsibility for ourselves, we change a fundamental part of our personalities. Each healthful habit we acquire, each muscle that we learn to relax, changes who we are. Let us begin with the breath.

Breathing

Most of us are shallow breathers and it is important that we change this so our bodies get enough oxygen. When we do not breathe deeply enough, we often feel dizzy, tired, and fearful. It is also important to exhale as fully as we inhale. It may be helpful to count your breaths or focus on the sound of your breathing.

Learning to focus on our breath and be more aware of our breathing calms the body and spirit. This kind of training is the basis of stress reduction, meditation, methods of dealing with pain and childbirth, as well as most forms of self-hypnosis. To learn to breathe properly is to allow life to enter into us, as opposed to marginally participating in life. To breathe deeply involves trust and letting go of the need to protect ourselves. Good breathing is a habit that is acquired over time by awareness and practice. It is also a habit that we can practice inconspicuously anywhere, anytime.

Rest and Relaxation

Our bodies and minds also need rest, a time to rejuvenate ourselves. Rest does not necessarily mean sleep, as quiet contemplation or relaxing activity can restore us even more than sleep itself.

Sleep and rest are even more necessary than usual if we are under stress. Sleep can provide the necessary outlet of dreaming, which is very important to mental health. Studies have shown that when individuals are allowed to sleep, but not dream, they eventually show signs of psychosis. It is interesting to note that some of the drugs used to treat depression affect the dream cycle and allow individuals to dream more. But in dealing with depression, it is important that sleep not be used as an escape from reality.

Meditation helps the body to relax and quiets the chatter in the mind. This can be achieved through using the breathing exercises mentioned earlier while quieting the mind. Regular meditation is a wonderful habit to acquire.

Other forms of rest or relaxation include walking, listening to music, reading a good book, and taking a hot bath. Hobbies, games, and quiet conversation are also forms of relaxation. Drugs and alcohol may seem to help you relax, but you will feel more tired rather than relaxed after the fact.

Many people have difficulty justifying the time necessary to relax. These people feel in some puritanical way that to waste time is evil. The fallacy here is to assume that relaxation is wasting time. Is eating or breathing wasting time? Of course not, nor is rest and relaxation. Rest is an investment in our bodies and spirit to keep us running at our optimum efficiency. Such activity is necessary to reduce stress and avoid disease. The correlation between stress and disease has been clearly proven over and over again. It is time we pay attention to our bodies and take responsibility in preventing illness in our lives by giving ourselves rest and relaxation.

Exercise

Again, my purpose here is a gentle reminder. Our attitudes about women and exercise have changed radically in the past two decades. We have moved from the belief that "femininity" means physical weakness toward a belief that strong, physically active women are beautiful. This is a huge psychological jump for many of us who were discouraged from being athletic as children. Many of us were left with the impression (by overprotective parents and disinterested physical education teachers) that physical activity was not just out of the realm of most females, but somehow dangerous as well. This experience, or lack of experience, left many of us with a basic mistrust in our abilities to use our bodies as well as a general feeling of alienation from the sensation of our own physical power.

It has only been in the past few years that I have begun to challenge my physical limits via exercise and experience the invigorating sensation of energy that accompanies strenuous exercise. I used to resist because it had become one of those "shoulds" in my life that oppressed me and invited rebellion. I had been told I "should" exercise for my health and to improve my figure. Neither reason had any appeal for me. It was only by sheer accident that I found myself in a situation in which I was forced to increase my level of physical endurance on a daily level. After the initial resistance and helplessness passed, I found myself enjoying the experience of pushing myself physically. The firmness of muscles and the positive changes in my body were secondary to the sensation of power within my body.

Let me encourage you, particularly if you are feeling depressed or frightened, to exercise. If this is not a regular part of your life already, then I suggest you begin with dancing and walking. Dancing is a joyous way to exercise, something you can do at home or with others. Be sure and work toward that moment of pushing yourself beyond when you simply want to stop. Work for that period in physical exercise when you transcend exhaustion and find yourself recharged. Walking at a fairly fast pace is another excellent way to introduce your body and mind to the almost magical work of experiencing the power within you.

Body Therapies

The body is the beginning and the containment of the "self." The body, the physical manifestation of the self, is so basic, so important to the identity that any change in the body fundamentally affects the character. Because of this premise, a variety of therapies have been developed that work directly with the body. Pioneers of this form of therapy include Wilhelm Reich, Alexander Lowen, and Stanley Keleman. Some, but not all, of the body therapies are Rolfing, Bioenergetics, Lomi, Trager, and the Feldengras Method. Dance therapy, Aikido, and massage are all related to body therapy, and some theorists would include these areas into the realm of body therapy as well.

Generally, body therapy is based on the premise that through emotional and physical trauma, as well as the repression of emotions (including sexuality), the musculature of the body becomes chronically deformed with tension. This rigidity or muscular "armoring" greatly inhibits our ability to function, both physically and psychologically. The goal, then, of all body therapies is to release tension, relax chronically tight muscles, allowing whatever held-in emotions to surface so that the psychological and physical aspects of the individual will be freer, lighter, and better able to function efficiently.

Some forms of learning are best experienced rather than talked about. Body therapy is an experiential form of learning that is in many ways more powerful than traditional verbal therapy. It is an amazing process to feel the relationship between emotion and how our bodies react. The theory here is not limited to the concept that we feel tense because of unpleasant emotions. Rather, we learn our own peculiar form of muscle tension in reaction to early emotions and this tension becomes a habit. Eventually the tension feels normal. Our body is still reacting with a protective response though the outside stimulus, the threatening experience, is long past. In this way, we hold onto unpleasant experiences and emotions, bringing the past into the present. When we choose to repress emotions in the present, our muscle tension becomes more acute. Through body therapy, this muscular tension is released, which changes in very fundamental ways who we are and how we view our internal and external world. Through this experience we can learn to trust in our bodies, our emotions, ourselves, and reestablish the most basic relationship we have in our lives by returning home to ourselves.

Nutrition

There has been so much attention given to the area of nutrition in the past few years that none of us can plead ignorance any longer. Almost everyone who eats poorly knows he is mistreating his body. The purpose of this section is not to educate as to the basics of nutrition; rather, this section is meant to be a gentle reminder.

Food has a great deal of symbolic meaning in the lives of women. It reminds us of the security of our beginning and of our traditional roles as wife and mother. It reminds us of obligation and the desire to nurture. Food is also our enemy, the seductive solace that lures us farther and farther away from the bodies we dream of.

For our bodies/minds to work efficiently, we must feed ourselves properly. This is the bottom line; there is no way to get around it. What is proper for one body may not work for another's. Some of us need a large breakfast, others need the main meal at noon. Some of us need two meals a day, while others need six.

We can't let what is conventional repress our knowledge of what our bodies need to operate at their optimum. We must learn to pay attention to whims and cravings. If these cravings are destructive, we can try to find a positive substitute that satiates that need. Pay attention. Experiment. And learn.

People, when under stress, seem to gravitate to the worst of their nutritional habits. Like some premeditated attempt to sabotage ourselves, when life is at its worst, we begin to consume everything we normally avoid or ignore feeding ourselves altogether. When some of us face crises, we feel we don't deserve good food and go without it. Others face crises by attempting to console themselves with huge quantities of "junk food." Be wary of this tendency. When we are under stress, we need to be especially careful to eat well. This is one more way that we can take responsibility for our lives by nurturing ourselves, so that we can heal whatever wounds are left by the period of crisis, and move on.

Sexuality

Sexuality refers to more than genitals and sexual intercourse. Sexuality also means viewing ourselves as sexual beings as well as by gender. Sexuality is not a purely physical subject. There is no area of human behavior that forms as complete and complex tapestry of mind and body as the area of sexuality. In many ways, to place this subject in a chapter on our bodies is a bit of a misnomer. No doubt, this area needs much more attention as a vitally important part of the psychology of women than I will give it within the confines of this book. But in many ways we have been discussing sexuality throughout this book. Over and over again, we have been discussing the female experience and the heavy psychological price women often pay to be feminine in our culture today. This small section on sexuality is the culmination of a theme that has woven its way throughout this book.

As mentioned earlier, our sense of gender is established very early in life. It is one of the first things we know about whom we are. This is a critical bit of information. With this sense of gender will come a whole set of rules, experiences, taboos, expectations, and information that will form the foundation of the personality. We are female and male before we have a name, before we are born; before we experience anything, we are formed female or male.

Along with the development of our sense of gender comes the sensation of sexuality. Erections have been observed in infant males soon after birth. There is little reason not to believe that female infants (and most definitely toddlers) experience sexual feelings. Oddly enough, it will be only after many years of such feelings, as well as years of reprimands for touching "down there," that we learn what those feelings are. This gap in information forms the basis of a great deal of sexual confusion. This situation is compounded for females. First, females are discouraged from touching their genitals at all, usually with the suggestion that we are "dirty down there." This is quite different from the experience of the young male.

> Boys were praised for handling their penis when they were toilet trained, whereas girls were diverted from direct genital contact. If we allowed our hands to linger on our genitals long enough, we may have experienced the pleasure derived from touching the clitoris. But we never heard anyone else mention these pleasant sensations. As a result, we may have grown up feeling weirdly unique—as though no other girl did such things or felt such things. Feeling that we must be abnormal, immoral, we would make silent pacts with ourselves that we would touch ourselves just this time and never again; but we were forever breaking this promise to ourselves and to the omniscient God observing us from above.[1]

From these experiences, we began to disown our genitals and our sexual feelings. Once we were aware of what exactly we were doing (especially masturbating), many of us stopped altogether or continued with guilt.

Second, the young female is bombarded by the messages of the media and her society which is telling her that her primary role in life is that of attracting and pleasing men. She may meet this expectation with enthusiasm, preening by the hour and carefully practicing her "Lolita"-like smile. Or she may retreat from this culturally accepted exhibitionism with a great deal of embarrassment. Whichever the case, she will meet the changes of puberty with a great deal of anxiety. Already shackled with the Playboy image of the perfect body, she will wonder whether her body will be good enough. Also aware of her "responsibility" to keep men at bay, she will wonder whether her body will be too good. By the time her body has developed, she will have accepted the notion that her body (and sexuality) is merely an object that exists for the purpose of attracting men. Her body will not feel familiar or comfortable any longer. Her sexuality and sexual feelings will be something to be controlled or used for the purpose of gaining love and acceptance. In this way, she will have lost the most fundamental aspect of her being.

From puberty on, most women remain at war with their bodies and sexuality. At best, it is a "cold war," a stand-off of non-acceptance and self-consciousness. At worst, it is all-out hate manifesting itself in neurotic self-depreciation and insecurity, anorexia nervosa, obesity, or sexual dysfunction. Few women ever learn to feel pride in or comfortable with their bodies. Few women ever feel pride in or comfortable with their sexuality.

Beyond the physical aspects, women experience a peculiar socialization regarding their sexuality. Double messages abound as the developing woman is told to be flirtatious but not sexual, provocative but not promiscuous. She alone is given the responsibility to police the sexual arena. After being raised to be pleasing, nurturing, dependent, and submissive, after being told over and over again that having a boyfriend is all-important, this young, insecure female is expected to walk the line between being a whore or a "tease." For many years her experiences with heterosexual sex will be fraught with anxiety and the frustration of saying "no" in the face of desire. Eventually, when she does have intercourse, it will more than likely be because she needs to prove something. Maybe she needs to prove her love for a particular man. Maybe she needs to prove that she is an adult woman. Whatever the case, most women agree that their first sexual experiences were less than pleasant and rarely fulfilling. Few women have their first experience with intercourse without being ridden with guilt, self-doubt, and fear. After her first sexual experience (certainly after marriage) the tables turn once again. Now she is considered an experienced woman and is expected to be highly orgasmic as well as sexually sophisticated. After years of repression, guilt, control, and anxiety, she is somehow miraculously supposed to drop her "hang-ups" and become an abandoned, multiple orgasmic, sensuous woman.

Despite women's liberation, most women still feel that they owe sex to men. In fact, since the so-called sexual revolution, it is hard to tell which episode of guilt is the more intense, that of having sex or that of not providing sex. For women who are married or living with their lovers, the unspoken sense of "duty" is still very much alive. Few women feel at ease choosing not to have sex for whatever reason or (for no reason at all), especially for an extended period of time. We still have not rid ourselves of the belief that we owe our partners sex, that we are obligated to provide the necessary sexual outlet whenever they desire. Somewhere we maintain the belief that men cannot stand to be sexually denied and it is our responsibility to take care of them sexually.

When the desire to please, nurture, and placate is mixed with sexuality, the effects are often detrimental to sexual fulfillment. No doubt it is a healthy desire to wish to please a lover sexually. But if this involves having sex when the sexual desire is not there, or when sex becomes a performance, the essential element of honesty is lost. In the end, beyond any romantic or esoteric declarations, the act of sex is a physical act. To truly enjoy sex, to lose oneself to the moment of excitation and climax is the natural purpose of sexual expression (aside from the biological basics of procreation). When sexual expression is motivated from a desire to please, placate, "buy love," or out of a sense of obligation, the beauty of the expression is lost. Then it is a gift not given out of the joy of giving, but out of a desire that expects something in return or a martyr-like sense of self-sacrifice.

To reclaim our sexuality from the throes of guilt, duty, fear, and anxiety, we must begin by owning our sexual feelings and separating these feelings from our neurotic desire to placate and appease. We must also give up feeling responsible for the sexual feelings of others. The names and threats that have coerced us into sexual contact must be reexamined and fought. Names like "frigid," "selfish bitch," "tease," and "whore" need to be wiped clean from our minds. Threats like "I'll have to find someone else," and "you would if you loved me" must be challenged.

For sexual expression to fit into our lives comfortably and

naturally, it cannot be forced. Nor should we always wait for love or the "right man" to come along in order to let ourselves recognize and express sexual feelings. All too often we confuse sex with love because we have not learned to differentiate between the two feelings. The good girl/bad girl or madonna/whore complex has confused many women into believing that they were in love when they were, in fact, "in lust." To be sexually responsible, we must learn that sexual feelings are with us every day and that love is a fulfilling, comfortable relationship that is built over time.

Reclaiming our sexuality means we must begin to recognize our sexual feelings. Reclaiming our sexuality also means we must realize that we are sexual beings with real needs and desires. The geisha girl/pleasure object view of ourselves needs to be liberated and transformed.

It is important that we learn to be proud that we are women, complete in our own right. As we learn to love our breasts and hips and vaginas and bellies, the symbols of our womanness, we will begin to accept and love ourselves so strongly that we cannot be swayed by the media's half-starved, silicone-injected woman-symbol. For this symbol is not real or warm or round as a woman should be. Let us make peace with our bodies, nurture the very best in our physical beings, and learn to appreciate our sexuality. Let us love ourselves enough to come home to our bodies and reclaim the very core of whom we are.

chapter fourteen

Upkeep of the Spirit

"Faith is a quality of being: of being in touch with one's self, with life, and with the universe. It is a sense of belonging to one's community, to one's country, and to the earth. Above all, it is the feeling of being grounded in one's body, in one's humanity, and in one's animal nature. It can be all these things because it is a manifestation of life, an expression of the living force that unites all beings." [1] The force that Alexander Lowen's previous quote refers to could be defined as "spirit." The words "faith" and "spirit" mean a sense of belief and connectedness to life, to the past, present, and future as well as to the earth and the natural forces that govern it. Faith is a belief without proof, separate from the need to objectify or rationalize. Spirit is the energy of life, originally identified with the breath, which courses through our bodies and connects us to each other as well as to the earth. Faith implies risk. To have faith does not mean just to think or believe out of an allegiance to a doctrine; rather, to have faith is to trust and deeply know. Spirit is known and felt. Spirit implies energy, will, and the embodiment of life. Without these things we are lost, isolated, fearful, confused, and depressed.

"Without some faith that one's effort will be rewarded, the motivation to extend one's self would be lacking. Necessity is not a sufficient incentive. My depressed patients are under the same necessity to function as everyone else, but it fails to move them. They have given up; in effect, they have lost faith and have resigned themselves to die." [2]

Here Lowen links loss of faith with depression. Lowen personifies this loss of faith and its message via depression even more explicitly in the following quote. "When loss of faith occurs people also seem to lose the desire and the impulse to reach out, to extend themselves and to fight. They feel there is nothing to reach out to, nothing to fight for. And, like my depressed patients, their ultimate attitude is, 'What's the use?' " [3]

Experts from a variety of disciplines—social scientists, psychologists, theologians, and political scientists—have noted that as a culture we have lost faith. Through technology, greedy overemphasis of masculine values and unresponsive institutions, we have lost faith in ourselves, our values, and our community. To lose faith is to give up, to lack the motivation to go on, and to become submerged in helplessness, apathy, and depression. We have lost contact and belief in our feelings, our values, our bodies, our institutions, and even our future. In losing contact with these things we have lost faith, lost our sense of spirit, and ourselves. Without faith and spirit, many of the tools presented in this book become valueless. For it is an act of faith to seek change in ourselves. We must use our spirit, our drive toward growth and life in order to change. We embody our minds and bodies with their limitations, potential, and emotions. But we must embody our spirit as well, for it is our spirit that links us together, provides meaning to our lives and gives us the strength to transform crises into opportunity.

Women are especially vulnerable to "loss of faith," having been raised with values and myths that turned out to be not only untrue but destructive as well. We have been trained to wait, to support others at the expense of ourselves, to negate our needs, feelings, and creative energy. We have been taught to distrust ourselves, our bodies, and our personal power. In many ways we have been taught not to live our lives at all, but rather, submissively wait to die and be as useful to others as possible in the meantime. Sensing the society in which we live (and representing a majority of the population) has little positive to offer us, it is not unexpected that we would lose faith amidst the helplessness we so acutely feel. Seemingly unable to effect change or create what we need, our spirit weakens while our hope for a better future for ourselves dies and we are left with lives without meaning as well as a deep sense of loss.

To reinstill faith into our lives and to strengthen our spirit, we must rebuild the lost connections with ourselves, with others, with the life force and with our feminine spirit. Considering our positions in society as women and the addictive nature of helplessness, this is not an easy task. But it is a vitally necessary task if we are to have the hope and the spirit and the will to create a better world for ourselves and those yet to come. Such a task is also a supremely fulfilling act in our own behalf. Strengthening us and linking us together so that the deep sense of aloneness that we have so fruitlessly attempted to escape is finally filled with peace.

Reestablishing Lost Connections:
The Link to the Self

Many of us have lost track of whom we are and of what we think, feel, and value. Our "self" consists of many components. To begin with, there is the body, which contains the mind, emotions, and the energy of life. This energy is not stagnant. It moves, grows, and wanes. In the last chapter we explored the meaning of the body and the importance of reclaiming our sexuality. To make a connection with our bodies, to be "in" our bodies, means developing conscious awareness. When we learn to "check-in" regularly with our bodies, finding areas of tension, learning to relax muscles, developing a deeper, fuller breath, we can slowly release the blocks that have deadened our sense of our selves. Most people have blocks in specific areas that protect them from emotion and energy. Because these blocks consist of muscular tension, they lose a great deal of energy to their maintenance. People can learn to let go slowly of these blocks and, when this is achieved, find that they have more energy and feel lighter.

Take a moment and find the place in your body where you hold in your feelings. Perhaps it is your chest, jaw and neck, or abdomen. If you cannot locate such a place, imagine you are very afraid and see what happens. Where do you pull in? Now imagine you are very safe and secure. Where do you slowly let go a bit? Once you have located this area, you can work with it, talk to it, learn to let go bit by bit.

Faith in the body also includes physical exercise. Skiing, dancing, and diving all take faith. Many women have been trained not to take risks with their bodies. They lack faith in their capacity to be strong, to have endurance, to be balanced. Physical activity can help us learn to reestablish belief in ourselves via our bodies.

Beyond the body, the self consists of values, emotions, capacities, experiences, and a sense of personal history. To know ourselves we must know what we value and have faith in those values as well as the spirit to stick by them. If we act against our values, then we have acted against ourselves. It is important that we learn to define our values and learn to take the risk of standing by those values.

To trust in one's emotions is an act of faith. Especially in our culture, which considers emotions to be unimportant, it is difficult to follow what we feel. Yet our emotions are a sense, as much as seeing or hearing. Our emotions must be recognized, validated, expressed, or released. If we do not do this we pay a heavy price in physical and emotional "dis-ease" as well as an eventual loss of feeling anything at all.

To trust in ourselves is to believe in our potential and abilities. This faith means both recognition as well as a commitment to better ourselves and improve these capacities. To learn is to extend one's self and to risk failure. In learning, we transform ourselves from whom we have been to whom we want to be.

When we have faith in our experiences, we have belief in our wisdom. We learn from our past experiences and we are able to take that knowledge into the future only if we have faith in our wisdom. To believe in experience is to make a spiritual connection between our past, present, and future. With this connection we take the wisdom gained from the past and apply it to the present to create a better future for ourselves. Without this connection we become emotionally retarded, reliving the past like a broken record.

Experience can be a past that we choose to forget or an education and evolution. If we have faith in experience we can weather bad times well and turn pain into knowledge.

Some helpful tools for reconnecting with yourself:

1. Keep a journal—use it to record your feelings, thoughts, and bodily sensations and dreams.
2. Write your autobiography. In this way, along with your journal, you will have a sense of experience and continuity.
3. Write a list of your values, update them regularly, and make them into a poster for yourself.
4. Engage in an activity that will force you to develop more faith in your body.
5. Practice breathing more deeply and fully while consciously working at releasing muscular tension. Do this every day.
6. Try body therapy or massage to increase your body awareness.
7. Consider therapy as an educational experience to help you know yourself better and increase your ability to enjoy life. Seek a therapist who is concerned, nurturing, but potentially confrontive. Do not go to a therapist who seems disinterested, bored, or patronizing. Beware of therapists who act superior, who give medication without significant therapy, or who do little more than listen. Finding the right therapist may take some time. A good therapist will probably give you a fifteen-minute or half-hour initial interview for free if you request it in advance. Find someone with whom you are comfortable, but do not expect the experience of therapy to be comfortable. Therapy is meant to help you confront that which previously was too frightening to confront. Despite this, therapy is a good investment in yourself and in your future— probably one of the wisest investments you can make.

Reestablishing Lost Connections: The Link to Others

Each of us lives in a community with others and many of us live in families. Yet, often we cut ourselves off from those whose support we need and who need us. Humans are social animals who were meant to live in groups. We need to live together to create, to help each other. Loneliness and deep feelings of isolation plague our culture. Generations are cut off from one another as are races and classes.

We feel helpless to effect change in our communities and to create a better life or environment for ourselves. Yet in many ways all we need to do is reach out, to extend ourselves to others, and all of this can change. But we hesitate. We are afraid of being hurt, ignored, or rejected. So we continue to hide, relating on only the most superficial of levels with both strangers and loved ones.

We also live in a political community, a community in which we have extraordinary potential influence, if only we would use it. We live in a country where the people were given the power to govern themselves and in which less than half of the people choose to exercise that power. The rest sit passively or complain. The destiny of this country moves in directions that frighten us, but we ask ourselves, "what's the use?" So our helplessness grows.

What can we do about the family that doesn't talk anymore, the community that is slowly deteriorating, the country that causes us to lose faith and be afraid? We can do a great deal. If we think of institutions or groups of people as a person we can see that such a person needs energy and stimulation to grow. We have become lazy about infusing our institutions with energy. We have replaced the energy necessary to keep a family alive with television. Instead of nurturing, confronting, and having fun as a family, we expect the television to do it for us. As a community, instead of taking care of the needy ourselves or instituting private-funding programs, we expect that the government will do it for us. Somehow we expect the government to be aware and responsible on its own without our participation or communication. Through this irresponsibility, we have ignored and divided ourselves. We no longer see the needy and we shut the elderly away. We no longer know or care about the local issues at election time. When we ignore the needs of our families, communities, or country it is like ignoring the needs of our bodies—we become unhealthy and eventually betray ourselves by creating a social environment that demands a great deal and gives little or nothing in return.

To take part actively in our social structure is an act of faith because the motivation of this energy comes from the belief that humans can work effectively together for the common good. It takes spirit to do this. Because people are resistant to change, groups of people change slowly.

With our families, there is a fear that if we are open we will be hurt. We bury hurt feelings, which fester into resentment until our only desire is to avoid. But the workability of the family unit must be based on honesty. Love without honesty is a lie. If we show our families only what we think they want to see, then we are being false with them and lying about ourselves. To begin changing the family and infusing it with energy, we must begin with ourselves by giving of our time, emotions, and thoughts—both positive and negative. This implies that we have faith in the other individuals being able to handle this honesty. This also means that we have faith that conflict is a necessary and important part of love and growth.

We can reestablish our connection with our community in many ways. We can join organizations that help people. We can help a few individuals on our own. We can also form networks to help each other or create an "improvement" in our community. We can form a neighborhood babysitting cooperative or a network of career women who need support and encouragement from one another. If the community needs more recreation, a network or group can be formed to brainstorm ideas on making this happen. What is the return for this energy? A sense of personal power, of knowing we can make a difference, and a sense of closeness with others as we work together and, yes, even play together.

Finally, we can reconnect with our communities via political involvement. Each of us potentially can have a tremendous impact on local government. Even state or national government is not beyond our influence. The issues that we are concerned about more than likely concern many others. For those of us who are "not interested in politics," consider this famous quote by Hillel:

> *If I'm not for myself, who will be?*
> *If I'm only for myself, what am I?*
> *And if not now, when?*

Some Suggestions to Help You
Reconnect with Others

1. Form a network of friends. Focus on strong, intimate friendships.
2. Get involved in recreational activities that interest you.

3. Think about ways your community needs improvement and form a group or network to make that improvement.
4. Start small with everything, but work toward the grand.
5. Help a few needy people out regularly, such as an elderly neighbor or neglected child. Learn to say "no" so that you will feel free to say "yes."
6. Take risks with your family. Learn to be more honest. And turn that television off!
7. Work on a local level with established political groups to effect change on the national level.

Reestablishing Lost Connections: The Link to the Spirit of Life

There is a bond that connects us all to each other, to our history and future, to the earth and all living things. When we sense this bond and feel part of a greater being, there is a sense of release, peace, and energy. This feeling has been often described as being connected to God. To try and connect with a supreme being without this sense of connection with others and our planet leaves us empty, like a pleading child. True faith is not something we feel only at a particular place and time such as in church. Rather, true faith is being able to sense or feel our connectedness, our commonality with all living things at all times. This gives us a sense of belonging, of trust and peace that no other experience can bring.

Humans have created religion to inspire this feeling in people. But often religion, like other institutions, becomes sluggish and unresponsive to the genuine needs of the people. Ideally, the purpose of religion is to inspire or motivate the spirit, the conscious life force in us all. To inspire, religion uses ritual, prayer, sermons, gatherings, and even dogma. If these things work, and the dogma is a tool of the religion rather than the governing force, then the religion will grow or evolve to serve the people. If the dogma becomes all-important, then the religion becomes staid and judgmental, demanding that the people serve the religion. This has happened in a great many religions as well as many other institutions that humankind has created to serve its people. Without the conscious searching, improving, and control of the people, the institution begins to demand service from the people rather than serving the people. Because of this, many people have abandoned religion.

The dogma of religion is both a good tool to give people guidelines for living as well as a potentially negative element. The goodness of dogma is that it creates structure and meaning. The negative aspect is that it can be used to justify the subjugation of a race, class, or sex of people by another. Hitler and the Ku Klux Klan both used or use religion to justify their actions. When dogma is given too much power, it can become highly egotistical and destructive, using its religion to serve its hidden agenda of superiority. In this way, religion has abandoned the needs of many women.

For those of us who find our needs unmet, our spirit uninspired by existing religions, it is imperative that we do not abandon religion altogether. This is important for two reasons. First, as human beings, we need the inspiration of the spirit that religious symbolism and ritual are designed to give us. Second, it is important that we do not abandon religion because, if we do, the religions left will represent only the needs and values of a small group. If this happens (and some say it already has), the representative religions of our culture will not truly reflect our culture. Since religion has tremendous influence on our minds, values, and self-image, we cannot afford to entrust it to a small group. This country was based on diversity and it needs a wide variety of religions that represent the diversity of its population.

"I believe that it matters little what gods people worship, what beliefs they hold, as long as their faith is deep. The sustaining power of a faith does not lie in its content, but in the nature of faith itself." [4] Lowen's comment gives us permission to create deities, rituals, and symbols that inspire our spirits and faith in life. Perhaps this is the creative religious freedom that we have long been in need of.

Reclaiming the Feminine Spirit

Since the inception of Judeo-Christian religion, the dogma of both religions has supported the subjugation of women. Most of us take this for granted. We take for granted that women have been excluded from the governing bodies of most religions. We take for granted that women have been barred from the priesthood and only recently allowed to be ministers. We ignore that women have often been referred to as unclean, full of carnal lust, and responsible for original sin. We try and overlook that God is male.

We are told that God transcends sex and that the sex of Jesus is unimportant. But, of course, the "He's," "Him's," and "The Father" and "The Son" are very important, for nowhere can we find "The Mother" (except the Virgin Mary, who was the mother of Jesus but not the Mother–God) or "The Daughter."

Whether an individual woman or girl is religious or not, these words and images must have a profound effect. Religion speaks to the unconscious as well as the conscious, attempting to give us parental models whom we are to emulate. To emulate God or Jesus a woman must negate her womanness and her experience of being a woman. She may see herself as unworthy of emulating God and rather choose to see herself as the humble daughter, serving her male God with the same adoration and passivity she has bestowed upon her father and her husband. But she will never feel the sense of validation and sexual equality with God that her male counterpart will feel. The question one must ask is, "Is this truly what God meant for women or has our civilization used dogma in God's name to keep women excluded, passive, and humble?" If we are all made in God's image, then is some aspect of God female and in a sense, a "She?" This sounds almost blasphemous though. Not because it is untrue or evil, but because the themes of "malesness," masculine values, and male domination are such a strong part of Christian doctrine. This is also the case because, as a culture, we see females as weak, unimportant sex objects, and the feminine aspect of God as nonexistent.

This feminine aspect of spirituality is the missing link between our culture and religion. Essentially, the realm of the religious or spiritual is the realm of the feminine. This is a feeling, an un-scientific realm. The dogmas of *all* religions preach the feminine values of nurturing, cooperation, love, understanding, and morality. It is no wonder that religion has lost its influence in a society that worships purely masculine values and denigrates feminine values. Alexander Lowen equates the devaluation of the feminine principle as a major cause of depression today.

"It is true that the patriarchal principle is today in a stage of crisis. It has become so overextended by science and technology that it may be on the verge of collapse. But until this happens and until the matriarchal principle is restored to its rightful place as an equal but polar value, we can anticipate depression will become endemic in our culture." [5] If the imbalance between these two principles is destroying our society and causing depression in all humans, then we can imagine that loss of value of the feminine aspect must cause an even more devastating depressive condition in women.

Again balance is the key. Each of us must find our own paths to the feminine spirit, woman and man alike. This is the spirit that teaches us of cooperation, nurturing, and the cycles of life. This is the spirit that reminds us of our connection to our planet and our responsibility to protect it. Our culture literally stands on the brink of disaster in search of (and oftentimes blindly ignoring) the essence and message of the feminine spirit.

For women reclaiming the true meaning of our feminine aspect is the most essential step toward reclaiming personal power and developing pride. There is a remembering that must be completed, a sense of the special heritage passed on from mother to daughter that reminds us of our connection to all persons, all things, and all time. Each act of our feminine aspect, from a luxurious bath, to a menstrual cycle, to giving birth, can be a ritual reminding us of that special connection.

In a very real sense we are beginning to redefine femininity itself. Slowly the passive clinging martyrdom of femininity is slipping away. What we are left with is something new that is beautiful, nurturing, and strong. We are also left with something ancient as well, something wild and wondrous which has never been wholly forgotten.

Reaching Back Through Time to Matriarchal Religion

There was a time when the feminine element was worshipped and god was a woman, known as the Great Mother Goddess, the Goddess of a Thousand Names.

It was not long before the various pieces of evidence fell into place and the connections began to take form. And then I understood. Ashtoreth, the despised 'pagan' deity of the Old Testament, was (despite the efforts of biblical scribes to disguise her identity by repeatedly using mascuine gender) actually Astarte—the Great Goddess, as she was known in Canaan, The Eastern Queen of Heaven. Those heathen idol worshippers of the Bible had been praying to a woman God—elsewhere known as Innin, Inanna, Nana, Nut, Anat, Anahita, Istar, Isis, Auset, Ishana, Asherah, Ashtant, Attoret Attar, and Hator—the many named Divine Ancestress. Yet each name denoted in the various languages and dialects of those who revered her, the Great Goddess. . . .

Even more astonishing was the archeological evidence which proved her religion had existed and flourished in the Near and Middle East for thousands of years before the arrival of the patriarchal Abraham, first prophet of the male deity Yahweh. Archeologists had traced the worship of the goddess back to the Neolithic communities of about 7000 B.C., some to the Upper Paleolithic cultures of about 25,000 B.C. From the time of its Neolithic origins, its existence was repeatedly attested to until well into Roman times.[6]

This religion was based on the seasons of year, the closeness with nature and reverence for birth, death, and rebirth. This was a religion that worshipped the manifestation of the Goddess in each human and in nature. The Goddess had a male aspect, known by many names, who was represented at times as her partner (consort) and at times as her male child. Women were considered to have a special wisdom. They were "priestesses, diviners, midwives, poets, healers, and singers of songs of power." These women of wisdom were known as wicce or "wise ones," from which comes the word "witch." [7]

The Old Religion existed and evolved. Through the Mother Goddess, medicine, astronomy, and agriculture were born. Motherhood was revered and women were respected.

When Christianity first began to spread, the country people held to the old ways for hundreds of years. The two faiths coexisted quite peacefully. Many people followed both religions and country priests in the twelfth and thirteenth centuries were frequently upbraided by church authorities for dressing in skins and leading the dance at the pagan festivals.[8]

Many symbols of pagan religion were taken up by the church, so as to ease a transition. The evergreen, the egg, even the Easter Bunny, were borrowed from the Old Religion. Many a Christian holiday has a marked similarity in theme and timing to pagan holidays or sabbats.

But in the thirteenth and fourteenth centuries, the church began persecution of witches, as well as Jews and "heretical" thinkers. Pope Innocent VIII, with his Bill of 1484, intensified a campaign of torture and death that would take the lives of an estimated nine million people, perhaps 80 percent of whom were women and a large group of which were children. . . . An enormous campaign of propaganda accompanied the witch trials as well. Witches were said to have sold their souls to the devil, to practice obscene and disgusting rites, to blight crops and murder children.[9]

Beyond the church's influence or the witchburnings and torture, many believe practitioners of medicine, doctors, also instigated the trials so that the villagers would be left without midwives and herbalists who were strong competition in the times in which people deeply distrusted "medicine."

Eventually, the knowledge of the goddess and witchcraft began to disappear. Civilization found a new religion—science—and all knowledge of the ethereal was either stamped out or remade in the mold of Christianity. The memories, knowledge, and beliefs died except in a few hidden groups.

Today there is new interest in the Mother Goddess. Books, magazines, conferences, and meetings devoted to this topic abound as many women have found in the oldest of religions a belief that meets their needs and a deity that reflects their being. Many women have found what they had so long ago lost, a sense of spirituality that is truly feminine in nature and a sense of "herstory" . . . of continuity, of personal power, beautifully expressed in this ancient prayer.

THE CHARGE OF THE GODDESS

I who am the beauty of the green earth and the white moon among the stars and the mysteries of the waters, I call upon your soul to arise and come unto me. For I am the soul of nature that gives life to the universe. From me all things proceed and unto me they must return. Let my worship be in the heart that rejoices, for behold—all acts of love and pleasure are my rituals. Let there be beauty and strength, power and compassion, honor and humility, mirth and reverence within you. And you who seek to know me, know that your seeking and yearning will avail you not, unless you know the mystery, for if that which you seek, you find not within yourself, you will never find it without. For behold, I have been with you from the beginning, and I am that which is attained at the end of desire.[10]

Carol Christ, another contributor to and editor of the book *Womanspirit Rising*, offers an article entitled, "Why Women Need the Goddess: Phenomenological, Psychological, and Political Reflections," in which she suggests several psychological and political consequences of the modernday resurgence of Goddess worship. First, "Psychologically, it means the defeat of the view engendered by partriarchy that women's power is inferior and dangerous."[11]

"A second important implication of the Goddess symbol for women is the affirmation of the female body and the life cycle expressed in it."[12] In Goddess religion the cycles of the bodies of women are revered, as each cycle symbolizes a cycle of life. The symbol of the moon and its twenty-eight day cycle of waxing and waning is expressed in Goddess religion as a symbolic connection with the menstrual cycle. Moreover, the cycle of youth, maturity, and old age (meaning wisdom) is depicted in representations of the triple goddesses. "For the Goddess is also seen as the creator of all the arts of civilization, including healing, writing, and the giving of just law. Women in the middle of life who are not physical mothers may give birth to poems, songs, and books. . . ."[13]

"A third important implication of the Goddess symbol for women is the positive valuation of will in a Goddess-centered ritual, especially in Goddess-centered ritual magic. . . . The emphasis in the will is important for women, because women traditionally have been taught to devalue their wills, to believe that they cannot achieve their will through their own power, and even suspect that the assertion of will is evil."[14] "In a Goddess-centered context, in contrast, the will is valued. A woman is encouraged to know her will, to believe her will is valid, to believe that her will can be achieved in the world."[15]

Another aspect Christ points out about the significance of the

Goddess is that Goddess worship encourages us to reestablish our bonds with other women as well as the specific heritage of women. As we learn to see the energy of women and the spiritual basis of womanhood as positive, we can find new reasons to value each other and the "heritage" of women.

From this analysis it is evident that Goddess-oriented religion is a potentially therapeutic source of inspiration for women. It is a therapeutic source for men as well, who must come to respect their own feminine aspect if they are to survive emotionally and physically. Alexander Lowen tells us that "therapy and religion have in common the aim to give a person the sense of belonging, identity, the ability to express himself, and a faith in life." [16] Religion, if it is to serve the people, must be therapeutic. For many, Goddess-oriented religion is and will be a therapeutic answer to a long awaited need.

In closing, here is a poem to help you with your battle against depression and your quest for personal power.

CELEBRATION

You are woman
  The future of the world
  Whose vision sees the past,
  present, and future
  Who knows the meaning
  of all actions
  and is the carrier
  of the light.
You are woman
  Within your body is
  the cycle of nature
  the rhythm of the moon
  the movement of the ocean.
You are woman
  sensitive and alive
  wise beyond your years
  for in your blood runs
  the knowledge of your foremothers
  who were healers, rulers, witches,
  and warriors.
You are woman
  You have given birth

in fields, healed the sick,
worshipped the abundance
of nature, buried your dead
and grown strong.
You are woman
who has been bought and sold
raped and abused
suffered beyond all words
given until you were dry
and grown strong
You are woman
Who knows the power
of all your womanness
the importance of nurturing
and justice
who has been persecuted
throughout the ages
for owning your body,
spirit and power
for not yielding your life
and you have grown
stronger still.
You are woman
rich in emotions, the wise ones,
the teachers of the meaning
of life, death, love, and peace.
You are woman
wear your woman's body proudly
feel the energy, light,
heritage and responsibility within you,
know your power
rejoice and be free.

Suggested Readings

Burns, David D. *Feeling Good: The New Mood Therapy* (New York: William Morrow and Company, 1980).

Butler, Pamela E. *Self-Assertion for Women,* revised edition (New York: Harper & Row, 1981).

Chesler, Phyllis. *Women and Madness* (New York: Avon Books, 1973).

Dowling, Colette. *Cinderella Complex: Women's Hidden Fear of Independence* (New York: Summit Books, Inc., 1981).

Flach, Frederic F. *The Secret Strength of Depression* (New York: Bantam, 1975).

Fromm, Erich. *The Art of Loving* (New York: Harper and Row, 1974).

Kiev, Ari. *The Courage to Live* (New York: T. Y. Crowell, 1979).

Koberg, Don, and **Jim Bagnall.** *Universal Traveler: A Soft-Systems Guidebook to Creativity, Problem-Solving, and the Process of Reaching Goals* (Los Altos, California: W. Kaufman, 1976).

Lowen, Alexander. *Depression and the Body* (New York: Penquin Books, 1972).

Peele, Stanton, and **Archie Brodsky.** *Love and Addiction* (Signet, NAL, 1976).

Ross, Ruth. Prospering Woman (Mill Valley, California: Whatever Publishing, 1982).

Scarf, Maggie. *Unfinished Business* (New York: Doubleday, 1980).

Schiffman, Muriel. *Gestalt Self Therapy* (Self Therapy Press, 1980).

Shaw, George Bernard. *Selected Non-dramatic Writings of Bernard Shaw,* edited by Dan H. Laurence (Boston: Houghton Mifflin Company, 1965).

Stone, Merlin. *When God was a Woman* (New York: A Harvest/ HBS Book, 1976).

Notes

CHAPTER 5

1. Stanton Peele with Archie Brodsky, *Love and Addiction,* (New York, N.Y.: Taplinger Publishing Co., Inc.), p. 56.
2. Ibid., p. 24.
3. Ibid., pp. 50–51.
4. Isidor Chein, "Psychological Functions of Drug Use." In Scientific Basis of Drug Dependency, edited by Hannah Steinberg (London: J. and A. Churchill, Ltd., 1969), pp. 13–30.
5. Stanton Peele, *Love and Addiction,* pp. 52–53.
6. Ibid., p. 53.
7. Ibid., p. 56.

CHAPTER 6

1. Maggie Scarf, *Unfinished Business* (New York: Doubleday, 1980), p. 159.
2. Ibid., p. 159.
3. Frederic Flach, M.D., *The Secret Strength of Depression* (New York: Bantam Books, 1974), p. 111.

CHAPTER 7

1. Muriel Schiffman, *Gestalt Self Therapy* (Menlo Park, California: Self Therapy Press, 1980), p. 134.
2. Ibid., p. 136.

3. Alexander Lowen, *Depression and the Body,* (New York: Penguin Books, 1972), pp. 159–160.

4. Ibid., p. 136.

5. Ibid., p. 86.

6. Ibid., p. 57.

7. Ari Kiev, M.D., *The Courage to Live* (New York: Bantam Books, 1979), p. 38.

8. Lowen, p. 30.

9. Ibid., p. 31.

10. Ibid., p. 33.

11. Ibid., p. 135.

12. Chesler, *Woman and Madness* (New York: Avon Books, 1972), p. 44.

13. Scarf, *Unfinished Business* (New York: Doubleday & Co., 1980), p. 82.

14. Kiev, p. 41.

15. Ibid., p. 40.

16. Ibid., p. 39.

17. Kiev, p. 37.

18. Ibid., p. 39.

19. Pamela Butler, *Self-Assertion for Women,* rev. ed. (New York: Harper & Row, 1981), p. 28.

20. Ibid., p. 29.

21. Ari Kiev, p. 30.

22. Lowen, p. 28.

23. Ibid., p. 32.

24. Scarf, p. 322.

25. Ibid., p. 152.

26. Ibid., p. 70.

27. Butler, pp. 31–32.

28. Chesler, p. 44.

29. Butler, p. 33.

30. Schiffman, p. 133.

31. Lowen, p. 85.

32. Ibid., p. 27.

33. Ibid., p. 87.

34. Scarf, pp. 184–185.

36. Schiffman, p. 133.

CHAPTER 10

1. Dr. Pamela Butler, *Self-Assertion for Women,* rev. ed. (New York: Harper and Row, 1981), p. 70.

2. Don Koberg and Jim Bagnall, *The Universal Traveler* (Los Altos, California: William Kauffman, 1976), p. 24.

3. Ibid., p. 12.

4. Ibid., p. 33.

CHAPTER 11

1. George Bernard Shaw, *The Quintessence of Ibsenism* (1891) The Womanly Woman.

2. Erich Fromm, *The Art of Loving* (New York: Bantam Books, 1956), pp. 35–39.

CHAPTER 12

1. Phil Laut, *Money Is My Friend* (San Francisco, California: Trinity Publications, 1979), p. 41.
2. Ibid., p. 6.

CHAPTER 13

1. Lonnie Garfiield Barbach, *For Yourself* (Garden City, New York: Anchor Books/Doubleday and Company, 1976), p. 21.

CHAPTER 14

1. Alexander Lowen, *Depression and the Body* (New York: Penguin Books 1972), p. 219.
2. Ibid., p. 219.
3. Ibid., p. 196.
4. Lowen, p. 196.
5. Ibid., p. 254.
6. Merlin Stone, *When God Was a Woman* (New York: Dial Press 1976), p. 9-10. Copyright ©1976 by Merlin Stone. Reprinted by permission of Doubleday & Company, Inc.
7. Starhawk, "Witchcraft and Women's Culture," *Womanspirit Rising,* edited by Carol P. Christ and Judith Plaskow, p. 260.
8. Ibid., p. 261.
9. Ibid., p. 262.
10. Starhawk, *The Spiral Dance,* p. 77.
11. Carol P. Christ, "Why Women Need the Goddess: Phenomenological, Psychological and Political Reflections" *Womanspirit Rising,* edited by Carol P. Christ and Judith Plaskow. This selection was originally published in *Heresies,* 2, no. 1 (1978).
12. Ibid., p. 279.
13. Ibid., p. 281.
14. Ibid., p. 282.
15. Ibid., p. 284.
16. Lowen, *Depression and the Body,* p. 214.

Index